MYRA'S MEN

Building the
Kettle Valley Railway

Myra Canyon to Penticton
by
MAURICE WILLIAMS

Foreword by Barrie Sanford,
author of *McCulloch's Wonder*

Published by the Myra Canyon Trestle Restoration Society
Kelowna, British Columbia
2008

Myra Canyon Trestle Restoration Society
Capri P.O. Box 22095, Kelowna, BC V1Y 9N9
www.myratrestles.com

Cover photographs courtesy of Penticton Museum & Archives

Cover and interior design by Donna Szelest

Distributed by Sandhill Book Marketing, Kelowna, BC.
To order, phone: 1-800-667-3848; email: info@sandhillbooks.com
www.sandhillbooks.com

Printed and bound in Canada by Hignell Book Printing

National Library of Canada Cataloguing in Publication Data

Williams, Maurice
        Myra's Men : Building the Kettle Valley Railway, Myra Canyon to Penticton
        / Maurice Williams; foreword by Barrie Sanford.

        Includes bibliographical references and index
        ISBN 978-0-9809878-0-5 (paperback)
        ISBN 978-0-9809878-1-2 (hardcover)

    1. Kettle Valley Railway—History. 2. Railroad construction workers—British Columbia—History. 3. Railroad construction workers--British Columbia—Social conditions. 4. Railroad construction workers—British Columbia—Social life and customs. 5. Railroads—British Columbia—Okanagan-Similkameen—History. I. Title.

HD8039.R3152C3 2008   385.09711'5   C2008-902438-9

To the Navvies, Blanketstiffs, Stiffs,
Camp-men and Boomers,
the men who built the KVR

TABLE OF CONTENTS

MAPS

FOREWORD

Nearly a century has passed since civil engineer Andrew McCulloch left Montreal in June of 1910 to direct the construction of the Kettle Valley Railway across the rugged mountains encompassing the western half of southern British Columbia. The story of that construction - and the political and corporate posturing that preceded it - is a fascinating one. It was the fascination of this story that prompted me to write my book *McCulloch's Wonder* more than 30 years ago. That book was the first historical work about the Kettle Valley Railway. But it certainly wasn't the last. In the succeeding three decades more than 20 books and videos have been produced with the Kettle Valley Railway as their subject. All of the creators of these works, like me, have succumbed to the inexplicable magnetism of this remarkable railway.

It is only natural that these historical works have focused on the corporate and political decisions that led to the railway's construction and choice of route. After all, in that pre-automobile age, decisions on railway routing determined which pioneer communities would grow and prosper and which would wither and be forgotten. But these works have told only part of the story. The Kettle Valley Railway was constructed in an age before extensive mechanization. Although barely one human lifespan has passed since its creation, the Kettle Valley Railway was constructed using technology more akin to that which built the pyramids 5,000 years ago than with our modern age. A few power drills and steam shovels were utilized at points of easy access, but the contribution of these machines was minor compared with that of the more than 10,000 labourers using only picks, shovels and pushcarts or wheelbarrows.

Most of the preceding historical works on the Kettle Valley Railway have acknowledged this reality, even if only in passing mention. But Maury Williams is the first to analyze these labourers in detail - who they were and what kinds of lives they led - by examining the men who built one portion of this railway, through Myra Canyon and across the Okanagan Highlands on to the east side of Okanagan Lake. His has not been an easy task. Written records are scarce and seldom revealing. Most of the labourers were illiterate, so they left no diaries or letters. And racial prejudices in that less-inclusive age precluded timely acknowledgment of the contributions made or the dangers encountered, by these predominantly immigrant workers. Considering the meager tools with which he has had to work, Maury has done admirably well.

While Maury's contribution is a genuine and valued addition to the story of the Kettle Valley Railway, the real record of the accomplishments of this forgotten army of workers is the railway roadbed itself. Like the ancient native tribesmen who, lacking written language, left their pictograph records carved in stone, so too the illiterate navvies of the Kettle Valley Railway have left us a legend carved in the rocks of southern British Columbia. Fortunately, the railway roadbed has been largely converted into a hiking and biking trail — the TransCanada Trail — so that roadbed is accessible from many different communities. And at both the Quintette Tunnels near Hope and Myra Canyon near Kelowna, provincial parks have been created, solely because of the former railway. Thousands of visitors now annually marvel at this permanent monument to the railway and its creators.

I encourage you to read this book thoughtfully and then walk the roadbed and trestles of Myra Canyon - preferably with your children and grandchildren. You will be left with a new appreciation of those who first walked through this canyon and how your life has been made richer because of them.

Barrie Sanford
Author of *McCulloch's Wonder*

THE
KETTLE VALLEY RAILWAY

It was not your typical railway. Instead of winding its way through the valleys, along the river banks and paralleling the mountain ranges like most railways, the Kettle Valley Railway (KVR) ran across the mountain ranges, down into the valleys and then up the other side again. Instead of avoiding steep grades, sharp curves, heavy snow and cold weather, the KVR faced all of these. Instead of traversing through a land rich in people and trade, it operated in a region in want of inhabitants; those who lived there were settled in communities no larger than a few thousand and most of them smaller than a few hundred. No wonder it was among the most expensive railways in North America.

Many thought it would never be built. They had not counted, however, on the determination of President James J. Warren or the ingenuity and resourcefulness of the chief engineer, Andrew McCulloch. At a time when most construction was still done by hand with pick, shovel and wheelbarrow, McCulloch built the Trout Creek Bridge, the Othello or Quintette Tunnels, the Adra and Belfort Loops and the Myra Canyon trestles, achievements which are testaments to his talents as a master railway builder. No wonder the KVR was and is, remembered as "McCulloch's Wonder."

The KVR was not just difficult to build, it was difficult to operate. In the winter massive amounts of snow caused slides and avalanches, particularly in the Coquihalla region, which meant closure of the line there for weeks. Springtime brought little relief as melting snow mixed with heavy rain caused washouts and rock slides, forcing long delays in service. Miraculously the railway never suffered a fatality of a paying passenger, although sadly train crews sometimes perished.

Today, of course, there are no longer trains on these tracks.[1] The KVR was unable to compete with trucks and cars on the new highways and it was unable to overcome the reluctance of travellers concerned about the time it took to journey to their destination by train. Efforts to promote tourism through the surrounding scenery or to concentrate on freight were to no avail. In 1989, nearly 75 years after the first train ran the distance from Midway to Hope, the last KVR cars travelled the tracks.

Yet it is remembered as a great achievement in railway construction and it is seen as an example of the determination of men such as McCulloch to triumph over the most difficult natural obstacles. But shouldn't we also remember those who toiled to make this "wonder" real? We should remember those with the pick and shovel, the wheelbarrow and the rough hands, and those who drilled out the tunnels, generally by hand, at the rate of five feet a day. We should remember those who have been overshadowed by the more well-known railway personalities. We should remember those other heroes: the labourers of the KVR and other Canadian railways.

This book looks at these forgotten men, the "navvies" and their immediate bosses. It answers many questions. Who were these workers who prepared the grade, assembled the trestles, laid the ties and spiked the steel? Where were their homes? Where and how did they live? What did they eat and where did they sleep? What was their work like and how much were they paid? What did they do when they weren't working?

Because of its uniqueness and the attention received with the 2003 fire, Myra Canyon serves as our initial focus in exploring the life of those who toiled to build the railway. However, in order to understand these men and their work, we have to appreciate the larger setting of the KVR. We need to recognize where the idea for its construction came from and how the planning and implementation progressed. The life of the navvy can not be understood outside this context and setting for his labours. The first chapter therefore gives an overview of the KVR, especially for those unfamiliar with its conception, construction and operation. It shows the considerable cause for building a railway from the southern interior to the coast. This broad picture is then augmented in chapters two and three by considering the venue for this particular story, the picturesque Myra Canyon and the route west to Penticton. By looking here at the planning, the clearing and the grading, the building of trestles and tunnels and the laying of the rail, the place and role of the navvy becomes even more evident. We see how he fits into the larger picture of making this section of the dream, as with the other sections of the KVR, into a reality. With this context firmly in mind, in the second half of the book we examine the navvy's day-to-day life. By looking at his origins, his camps, his work and his leisure, we come to better appreciate the navvy as a vital part of the Canadian story. These men of Myra and the hundreds like them on the KVR deserve our recognition and our respect. This book is a step in that direction.

---

[1] There is one exception. The Kettle Valley Steam Railway Society in Summerland operates a steam locomotive with several vintage passenger cars and a caboose. The train takes tourists over a short stretch of the line.

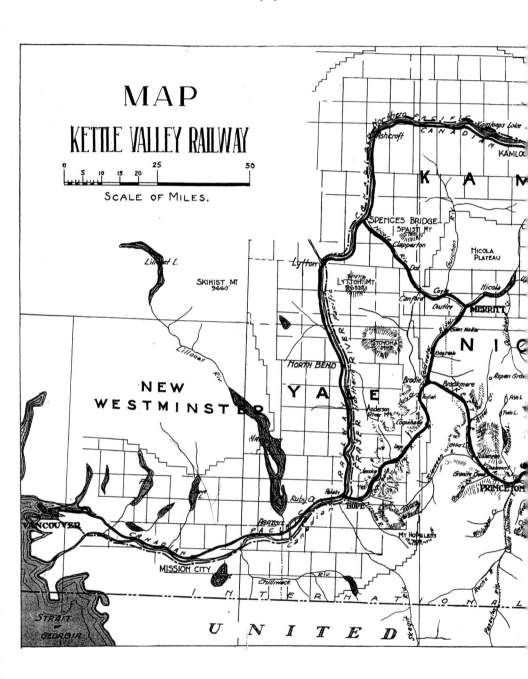

13

CHAPTER I

THE KVR:
DESIGN AND CONSTRUCTION

The KVR entered into British Columbia's history at the end of a long period of railway building in Western Canada. To entice BC into confederation, the government of Canada promised a railway in 1871 to bind the Dominion from the Atlantic to the Pacific. The Canadian Pacific Railway (CPR), the answer to that pledge, was born. Building the CPR across the prairies was not particularly easy, but getting the line through the mountains in the west turned into a major challenge. In choosing a route the engineers finally swung through Banff, negotiated the Kicking Horse and Rogers Passes, passed through Revelstoke and Kamloops and then moved south following the Fraser River down to Vancouver. In 1885 CPR officials drove the last spike and Alexander Ross snapped his famous photograph at Craigellachie, near Revelstoke, BC.[1]

This route, which made the most geographical and political sense for the CPR, left the southern interior of British Columbia quite isolated. Residents there had hoped for a rail line following the old Dewdney Trail, with its connections to the coast. Instead they were forced to trace a long roundabout route, north by lake steamer or south by stage before they could link up with a rail line. It was generally a two day journey to the coast.

Two years after the ceremony at Craigellachie, however, when the applause had ceased, two Americans found silver in the Kootenays in the shadow of the Rockies and took a rucksack of the rich ore to Butte, Montana. Soon thousands of Americans stampeded north into the isolated corner of BC and rapidly staked hundreds of mining claims in the Kootenay region. Those were heady days, as the men built their new communities around the mines, adding, of course, numerous saloons, ladies of the night, an opera house or two and the occasional church. But more importantly, the miners used the fastest and cheapest way to bring up their supplies – from the railway to the south and the link through Spokane. They recognized that it was also far easier to ship the valuable ore south via this same

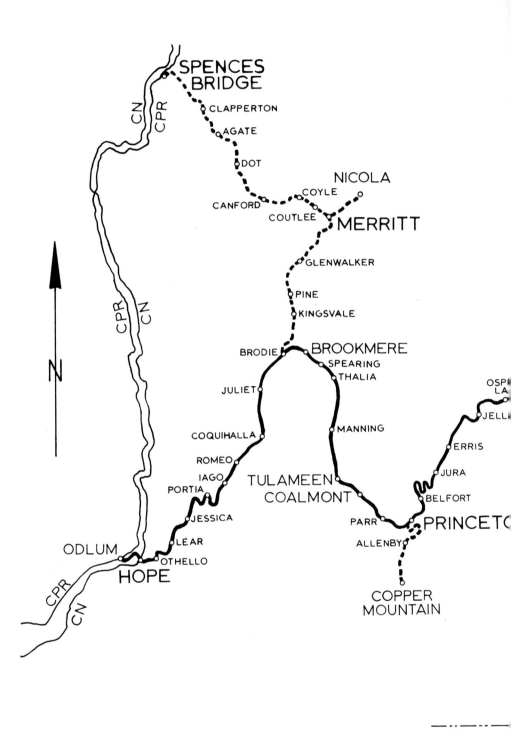

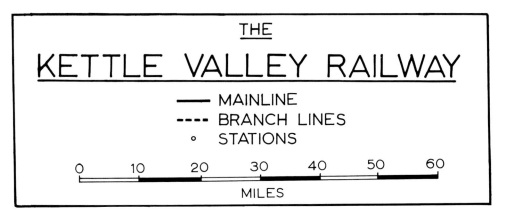

THE
KETTLE VALLEY RAILWAY

——— MAINLINE
- - - - BRANCH LINES
  ∘ STATIONS

0   10   20   30   40   50   60

MILES

CN

KELOWNA

RUTH   MYRA
LORNA   McCULLOCH

CHUTE
LAKE   COOKSON
GLENFIR
                LAKEVALE
ADRA
ARAWANA
WINSLOW   LOIS
THIRSK   CARMI
KIRTON   BEAVERDELL
CRUMP
FAULDER   DELLWYE
WEST SUMMERLAND
                TAURUS
SKAHA
PENTICTON   RHONE
KALEDEN   WESTBRIDGE
                ZAMORA
OKANAGAN
FALLS   KETTLE
McINTYRE   VALLEY
DLEY
OLIVER   ROCK
GN   HAYNES   CREEK   CPR
ELLIS
OSOYOOS   MIDWAY
OROVILLE

17

James Warren, President, and Andrew McCulloch, Chief Engineer of the KVR, posing after the completion of the railway. *Barrie Sanford Archives*

American line. BC's southern interior essentially became a commercial annex of the United States and there was some danger of political annexation. It did not take government officials long to realize that the Dominion needed a second railway to preserve its sovereignty in this region as well as to retain the valuable mining revenues. As a consequence, the dream of a Kootenay-to-coast railway was born to keep the area and its wealth firmly in Canadian hands. It was out of this dream that the Kettle Valley Railway emerged.

One of the more aggressive lines pushing into the Kootenays to access the boom was the Vancouver, Victoria & Eastern (the VV&E), a subsidiary of the Great Northern (GN) owned by Canadian-born American railway magnate J. J. Hill. Described as "the barbed-wire, shaggy-headed, one-eyed old son-of-a-bitch of Western railroading," Hill fought everyone and everything as he extended his interests across the continent.[2] At one time the GN had multiple lines crossing into Canada, eagerly transporting BC ore south.

Rivalry between Hill and the CPR dated back to the building of the Canadian Pacific when Hill was one of its executives and had disagreed with General Manager William Van Horne's decision to route the line north of Lake Superior. Hill had left the CPR in a fury, swearing, "I'll get even with him if I have to go to hell for it and shovel coal!" Van Horne would reciprocate, asserting that the CPR planned to "mop the floor with the Great Northern or any other American company extending its lines into the Northwest."[3] In the 25 years after 1893 the battle between the two railway giants involved a plethora of railways. When Hill and Van Horne grew old, the battle continued between J. J.'s son, Louis, and the CPR's new general manager, Thomas Shaughnessy. This long-standing rivalry added cause for the KVR to be built.

One of the small railways that sought to exploit the area's mineral wealth, this time from British Columbia, was the Kettle River Valley Railway (KRVR). The Canadian group that chartered it in 1901 intended to connect the ore smelter in Grand Forks, BC with a mine at Republic, Washington, 30 miles south of the border. "Like mice challenging a cat" the KRVR confronted Hill's plans for domination of Washington state with the Great Northern Railway. The little company put up a good fight, but by 1907 Hill had all but destroyed it.

In 1908, James John Warren, an Ontario lawyer who had taken over the almost defunct Kettle River Valley Railway, attempted to salvage what he could. The man he thought might help was the CPR's Thomas Shaughnessy. Unable to reach the CPR boss any other way, Warren took passage on a steamer across the Atlantic on which he knew Shaughnessy would be a passenger. Warren also knew that Shaughnessy had personal business interests in BC, including the Summerland

PRAISES FOR J. J. WARREN

Premier Richard McBride's New Year Message, 1913

Mr. James J. Warren, the president of this system [KVR], has shown himself since the inception of construction operations, indefatigably active in pushing his great work forward, going ahead of his exact obligations under the agreement with the province and leaving no doubt in the minds of anyone as to his sincere desire to have this road completed and catering to the transportation necessities of British Columbia just as soon as possible. Unless there should come some setback not at present to be anticipated on any ground whatever, one may look to see the entire Kettle Valley system completed and ready for operation by the end of 1914, bringing the Coast and the Kootenays into close and beneficial touch commercially and greatly stimulating the exploitation and utilization of an important section of the province that up till now has lain dormant, awaiting the magic key that railways bring.

Vernon News, January 2, 1913

Development Company which helped make Okanagan fruit world-famous. The two met on board. Soon their discussions led to a proposed partnership whereby they would build a line from Midway, where the CPR tracks from the east ended, to Merritt and on to Hope. For Shaughnessy it meant he would expand the CPR's trackage in southern BC, tap the wealth residing there, keep the region under Canadian sovereignty and most importantly, counter Hill who was determined to take the VV&E all the way to the coast and exploit the wealth himself. For Warren it meant financial salvation and invigoration of the KRVR.

Shaughnessy first met BC Premier Richard McBride, who after a remarkably brief discussion agreed to support the scheme.[4] Then, the CPR boss went to Montreal to present the plan to his board of directors. They were unenthusiastic, offering all sorts of objections about the terrain, the climate and the economic wisdom of such a line. Facing what seemed like a unified opposition, Shaughnessy may have hesitated, but if so, it was not for long. Showing the same vision and fortitude of his predecessor, William Van Horne, he asserted: "Gentlemen, the people of Canada want an all Canadian line and I am going to give it to them."[5] When his opponents said nothing, Shaughnessy interpreted their silence as consent and proceeded with the plan. As a result, his partner in the scheme, J. J. Warren, became the front man, president of the renamed Kettle Valley Railway in 1910 and the project was on.

One of the first tasks that Warren faced was to find someone to build the railway. He was competent to manage and direct the affairs of the KVR, but the job of constructing such a railway required the skills of a highly-talented engineer. When he discussed the problem with Shaughnessy, the CPR boss had no hesitation in naming Andrew McCulloch, a man who would not only oversee the construction, but would direct its operations for more than 20 years. As Barrie Sanford, author of *McCulloch's Wonder*, wrote, "That man's name would become synonymous with 'The KV.'"

When Warren and McCulloch met, they formed a deep and abiding friendship and developed a most remarkable partnership. To Warren fell the task of organization, contracting, sorting out the logistics, obtaining the supplies and equipment, acquiring land and the rights-of-way, dealing with local interests and politicians and keeping in the closest contact with Shaughnessy. To McCulloch went the work of surveying the line and deciding its location across three mountain ranges, estimating the materials needed and determining those to be taken away, planning the many tunnels, multiple trestles and numerous cuts, overseeing the contractors and most importantly, finding a way to build over, through or

Andrew McCulloch, about 1916. This is the only known photograph of McCulloch taken during the construction era.

Barrie Sanford Archives

around the seemingly-impossible parts. His role was much more dramatic, but Warren's was no less important and the two men made a highly-effective and complementary team.[6]

In June 1910 McCulloch left his CPR post in Montreal and boarded a train for the west. Excited, enthusiastic, apprehensive and anxious – his diary showed all these emotions. Like many who accept new positions, he had some doubts about his ability to complete the task. It was a huge undertaking. Although he would persevere and eventually triumph, upon arrival he was not so sure. He found a host of problems. With his deadline to begin construction only days away, McCulloch lamented: "There were no engineers in sight ... certainly none in southern British Columbia. There were no responsible contractors near at hand and there was no time in which to get plans approved by the proper authorities. In fact, there were no plans to approve."[7] He had trouble finding unskilled labourers (he needed thousands in that age before mechanization). He found that steel mills had orders for rails dating back two years. There was a scarcity, if not an

ANDREW MCCULLOCH.

"That eccentric genius who strung a railroad from peak to peak across the mountains."   Saturday Evening Post

Born into a farming family in Ontario in 1864 he trained as an accountant but never pursued that as a career. He saw his opportunity as out west where he moved, eventually finding work, not in Vancouver, but in a lumber mill near Seattle. Some months later he began his railway career when he gained "a pretty good job," as he called it, with the Great Northern. When that experience ended, he eventually returned to the mill. Now it was that he had his opportunity to indulge in his love of Shakespeare and the theatre. He would row across Puget Sound in an evening to attend performances, then row back, arriving just in time for work. The names of several KVR stations reflect his love of Shakespeare.

Hearing that the CPR was hiring, in 1894 he secured work with the company, later moving on to Michigan where he gained more experience and promotion to resident engineer. Subsequently, he returned to British Columbia where he did survey work on Canadian Pacific's Crow's Nest line before moving on to the Kicking Horse Pass. Here he distinguished himself with brilliant work on the spiral tunnels, an achievement which led to his appointment as a Division Engineer of Construction for the CPR in Montreal.

In May 1910, when Thomas Shaughnessy approached him about the KVR, he was 46 years old. He immediately accepted the job as Chief Engineer, both for the challenge and because of his love of the west and the out-of-doors. He, his wife Annie and their four children moved to Penticton. After completion of the Kettle Valley Railway he remained as its chief engineer until his retirement in 1939. He died in 1945 at age 81. He was buried in Penticton's cemetery.

Although he had some misgivings about the KVR project, calling it "rather ambitious," his daughter Ruth later wrote: "There is no doubt that the Kettle Valley Railway was his favourite piece of work."

unavailability of rolling stock and locomotives. It seemed everything to build a railway was either out of stock or in short supply.

Exhibiting the same traits which had already earned him his various promotions and commendations, McCulloch again showed himself to be a man of some determination and purpose. He found his engineers, he located some men, he scrounged materials, he tracked down equipment (including a locomotive) and he started constructing a railway. Work began first at Midway, moving west along the Kettle River towards the Okanagan. Then grading and tracklaying commenced at Merritt, moving south. In 1912 a third segment was started at Penticton, with the activity proceeding both east and west from there. By the beginning of 1913, over 2,000 men were labouring on the four segments and grading had extended 132 miles (212 km). Headquarters and maintenance facilities had been set up in Penticton and track was laid for 85 miles (137 km), including seven miles (11 km) to Trout Creek. This was reasonable progress, although 80 per cent of the railway remained to be completed.

Fortunately, some labour and financial problems were eased. In 1912 the Canadian government relaxed the restrictions it had placed on workers from other countries. That same year, the BC government subsidized that part of the line which would pass through and beyond the Coquihalla region. It provided a grant of $10,000 a mile for the track through the Cascade Mountains and offered $200,000 towards the bridge over the Fraser River at Hope (motorized traffic would use it as well as the KVR). Further, it gave the railway an exemption from taxation until July 1, 1924, plus a free right-of-way through Crown lands. This improved financial incentive was strengthened in 1913 with another $250,000 from the federal government for the Fraser River crossing.

A LASTING FRIENDSHIP.

J. J. Warren to Andrew McCulloch, 1937

Dear Chief,

I had a nice letter from you in December. There isn't anything you say appreciative of the years we were together that I won't agree with. In fact they were in many respects the happiest days of my life and you were the main factor in that happiness. It is not often that men of mature age become such friends as we did - and are. Those journeys together and the unexpected occurrences will never be forgotten and unfortunately cannot be repeated.... Then we used to speculate as to what in H-- would be carried by the railway and now see the loads go by.

Quoted in Beth Hill, *Exploring the Kettle Valley Railway.*

Despite the improvements and numerous public proclamations that the line was moving along, progress was really slow. Part of the reason was the extremely difficult terrain through which the railway travelled. Nowhere was this more evident than in the Coquihalla region. The first problem there was the winter snows. Four to five hundred inches (10 to 12.7 m) of wet snow was not unusual.[8] Any thaw meant slides followed by washouts and destroyed bridges and occasionally an entire hillside which slipped down into the canyon. Then there was a second problem. The Coquihalla Pass was so rugged and narrow that only a single railway track could get through and J. J. Hill, still battling the CPR, had already submitted right-of-way surveys for the pass. He seemingly had first claim on a line through the Coquihalla. Not surprisingly, a legal battle ensued, as each side tried to outmanoeuvre the other to obtain sole control of the right-of-way. Only when each side weakened due to a changed political climate and an economic slump in 1913 were the two forced to collaborate.[9] Hill's advancing age also helped bring about a resolution. The two companies agreed that the KVR would build and maintain the line through the Coquihalla and allow the VV&E to use the track in exchange for an annual fee. The VV&E, in turn, would grant the KVR running rights over its track between Brookmere and Princeton, thus saving the Kettle Valley crews from building a costly second line.

The problems in constructing the KVR never seemed to end. One of the issues for McCulloch was that he was supervising the construction of a railway across 300 miles (500 km) of wilderness. He had to move back and forth, often by horseback, regularly on foot and occasionally by boat. Frequently, he travelled by rail via Spences Bridge and Sicamous and at times took passage to the US, boarded a train and crossed back into Canada.

The Trout Creek trestle near Summerland under construction, 1913. The wooden trestle approach was awaiting the steel centre piece. The crane was used to drop the "bents" (the wooden vertical supports) into position and would soon place the steel in the middle. The bridge stood 241 feet above the creek level and was the highest bridge on the KVR. Steel and gravel fill later replaced the wooden trestles.

Penticton Museum

McCulloch and his work crews also faced significant engineering obstacles. One important impediment between Penticton and Princeton, for example, was the Trout Creek gorge near Summerland. It required a major effort to cross, including a second start when a flood wiped out the preliminary staging. The KVR engineers spent days there surveying and struggling with their plans. At one point, McCulloch himself resurveyed the entire canyon when an argument arose regarding the bridge measurements. It was a tribute to his skills that when the bridge was lowered into place, it was only ¼ inch short of a perfect fit. Completed finally in October 1913, the bridge was one of the longest and highest of its kind in North America.[10]

McCulloch was not finished with the difficult Coquihalla region either. It required numerous bridges, any number of snow sheds and thousands of feet of tunnels. The greatest single challenge was where the Coquihalla River entered

These two photographs provide a graphic perspective of the Quintette Tunnels before and after completion of the KVR. The upper photo looks through the west portal of tunnel 12 with tunnels 11 and 10 visible through the opening. The Coquihalla River is on the left. The photo on the right, taken in virtually the same spot by Frank Palmer of Spokane in late summer of 1917, shows the same tunnels after completion of the line. The rail sits on a deck truss bridge. *Barrie Sanford Archives*

a narrow canyon with sheer granite cliffs 300 feet high (95 m) just east of Hope.
Here the river made an abrupt hairpin turn making it impossible for the railway
to follow the river, even if there had been room. Many thought it best to avoid
the route altogether or if necessary, drill and blast a mile-long tunnel, but not
McCulloch. He lowered himself down the cliff face in a basket to survey the route
and found that it was possible to drill not one but four tunnels, one of which would
be "daylighted" or opened up on one side, giving the impression of five tunnels
(i.e., the Quintette Tunnels). Most amazingly, the "five" tunnels and the two
bridges across the Coquihalla River at that point were constructed in a perfectly
straight line.[11]

Between Midway and Penticton, the primary interest in our account, McCulloch
faced two other important challenges. One worry was the Chute Lake region just
north of Naramata. The problem here arose when, for financial reasons and
because of changes due to difficult terrain further east, he decided to change

The Glenfir Loop east of Penticton, early 1950's. This loop was part of Andrew McCulloch's plan to
overcome the near impossible 4.5 per cent grade coming out of Chute Lake pass to Penticton. It enabled
McCulloch to achieve a grade of 2.2 per cent, considered the maximum grade for mainline track.

Barrie Sanford Archives

the route of the original survey. Instead of going around Okanagan Mountain he chose to use the pass at Chute Lake. But in so doing, he encountered a virtually impossible 4.5 per cent grade into Penticton. After tramping over the ground for some days McCulloch came up with an ingenious idea. He proposed a double loop, building a 2.2 per cent grade out of Penticton to Glenfir; doubling back five miles (eight km), maintaining the same grade; then doubling back again, this time passing through a 1,600 foot long (490 m) horseshoe shaped tunnel, eventually ending near Chute Lake. It was after accomplishing this feat that his engineers started calling the KVR "McCulloch's Wonder."

His other challenge was the spectacular Myra Canyon. Not only was this section long at nearly six miles (10 km), it was deep at 705 feet (215 m) and it split into two parts at the south end, creating an east and west fork. The whole looked somewhat like the letter "W" on its side. "Never saw a railway built on any such hillside as this! Cannot even guess the cost now," McCulloch wrote in his diary after an early visit.[12] Upon closer examination he saw that a great deal of stone abutment work, more than a few trestles and several tunnels would be required to get around the canyon. Individually, each piece of work was not unusual, but the total effort in such a small space was daunting, not to mention costly.

McCulloch successfully addressed these issues just as he did his other major challenges. Along with his engineers, the contractors and their navvies, he planned and built 19 wooden trestles, two of which were major structures across the forks of Canyon Creek. In addition, they drilled three tunnels, although one was eventually "opened up" and became a major rock cut. What made this construction complex and time-consuming was the terrain. It was so remote and rugged that the trestles could not be constructed until the tracks were laid to the edge of each gap. It was just too difficult to bring the materials in by horse-drawn freighters. To speed things up McCulloch made use of pre-fabricated trestle bents, mostly framed in Carmi some 38 miles (61 km) away and transported them to the site ready for use. The trestles also had another interesting feature. McCulloch's insistence on accuracy, like his colleagues of the day, meant that no shims were permitted. The fittings had to be exact. When completed, the total amount of timber in these trestles was staggering: nearly four million board feet, plus 25 carloads of bolts and ironwork were used to hold the Myra Canyon trestles together.

The conquest of each challenge brought the KVR closer to completion and within a few years the promise of a line became a reality. The last spike on the Midway to Penticton section was driven on October 2, 1914. Only eight months later on May 31, 1915, the track from Midway to Merritt opened. Then, on September

An ink drawing by Willliam "Bill" Knox of a westbound passenger train on the steel bridge over the West Fork of Canyon Creek (today's trestle 6 over Pooley Creek, mile 87.9), ca. 1932. Knox was a member of the engineering staff who worked on the replacement of the wooden trestle with steel in 1932.

Barrie Sanford Archives

28, 1915, service commenced from Brodie to the Coquihalla Station. This meant only one section remained, that through the Coquihalla Pass. As much as Warren and McCulloch wanted to push ahead, however, they had to wait, delayed by a record snowfall of nearly 220 feet (67.7 m) that year. This provided a taste of future winters. Finally, on July 31, 1916, the line through to Hope opened and the rail was completed.

In September 1916 Warren and McCulloch joined Shaughnessy on a special inspection tour. As the three men sat on the open platform at the back of the train, they must have relished the newly-created rhythm – the clicky-clack of the track and the clatter of the trestles – and they must have admired the scenery as it slipped by. They surely experienced that great sense of accomplishment which follows a difficult project. They had made the dream of a Kootenay-to-coast railway come true. They had given the people of southern BC a direct link to Vancouver. They had thwarted the American dominance in the area, not to mention Hill, the VV&E and the Great Northern and they had ensured the region for Canadian sovereignty. All of this was no mean accomplishment. Against all odds they had built the KVR, which for many years to follow was the lifeline for people of the southern interior and its economic development.

Yet, in financial terms the success was questionable. The KVR made an operational profit carrying ore, coal, lumber, fruit, passengers, mail and general freight, but the $20 million debt for construction was never recovered. It also suffered from other things that limited even the operational profit. In the few short years it took to build the line, the world had changed. The first World War and its aftermath drained funds, labour and resources which were not replenished. Traffic demands changed and economic development plans were curtailed. The mines and smelters in the Greenwood, Grand Forks and Phoenix areas, for example, closed permanently as metal prices collapsed. The output from these facilities had figured prominently in the decision to build the KVR and now it was no more. Even the general freight and passenger traffic which had enriched the CPR and its Great Northern rival in the years prior to 1914 dropped dramatically.

Then came the other major considerations: maintenance and the great challenge of keeping a mountain railway open and running. It was tough work. In the winter the crews battled the cold and the snow. They contended with trains pushing through major snow storms, only to be cut off and isolated and then abandoned. In the summer the intense heat created another danger, that of forest fires. In the frightfully hot summer of 1931, for example, fires first threatened the bridges near Portia, then another blaze headed towards Brookmere from Juliet, while a third inferno did a great deal of damage to the line near Carmi. Only a short time after, another firestorm moved toward Myra Canyon with its spectacular and vulnerable wooden trestles. Tank cars loaded with water rushed

A crew battling the snow to extricate a locomotive at the tunnel near Romeo. The photo, taken about 1943, shows the perennial winter challenges in the Coquilhalla as the KVR struggled with "mountains of snow." *Barrie Sanford Archives*

to the site and crews, choking in the thick smoke, struggled to keep the wood wet. That same year saw the bizarre instance of a plague of grasshoppers that stripped some orchards clean, moved on to a section of nearby tracks, greased them up and stopped several trains.

It was also a dangerous rail line with its share of runaway trains, near-collisions and staggering wrecks, yet it had one of the best safety records on the continent. Part of the explanation for its phenomenal safety record lies with Andrew McCulloch. He supervised its operations closely and demanded meticulous attention to the company's safety procedures. He ensured that track cars or in winter a plow train, preceded the regular service through the Coquihalla Pass to look for slides or washouts. He maintained daily foot patrols checking the line and reminded train crews to test their brakes before undertaking every down-grade. Once a year McCulloch walked the line himself, inspecting every bridge and every tunnel. He would sit under the trestles and listen for the moans and groans as trains passed over. If there was plenty of creaking and squeaking all was okay, but if there was silence, it meant rot and punk and that brought speedy repairs.

For nearly half a century the railway served as an economic lifeline, hauling

A small salute to Shakespeare at Othello Station, just east of Hope, 1949. Andrew McCulloch, a great admirer of the English bard, named six of the stations between Hope and Brodie after Shakespearean characters. His designations are unique in the annals of railway lore of the British Empire.

Barrie Sanford Archives

freight and people and helping to develop the region. Then, better roads and air travel captured more and more passengers and cargo. In 1959 a disastrous November brought heavy rains, washing out sections of the Coquihalla line, and reinforced a decision to abandon the troublesome pass. By 1961 the rails were gone from that area. Within a year, passenger traffic on the rest of the line declined drastically and the CPR, which had taken over direct control of the KVR in 1931, lobbied the government for permission to end all passenger service. In 1964 the Penticton Branch of the Okanagan Historical Society took the last and very quiet ride eastbound to Rock Creek. Freight trains continued for a few more years but the trains grew shorter and the profits slimmer. By May 1973 trains stopped completely between Midway and Penticton. Then the Penticton station closed in 1985 and a short time later its roundhouse was dismantled. Finally, in 1989 the last train left Merritt for Spences Bridge. The dream which had become a reality was now only a memory of a distant era.

Yet the KVR is a memory very much alive today. It lives on in the wonder and attraction drawing the many visitors to the Quintette Tunnels. It exists in the regional park near Naramata with its construction-era stone ovens. It especially survives in the Myra-Bellevue Provincial Park and its portion of the TransCanada Trail. It is to this last area, the Myra Canyon locale, that we now turn, our next step in establishing the setting for the KVR navvies.

---

[1] I have avoided extensive footnoting except for quotations and explanatory and noteworthy information. The best and most complete account of the Kettle Valley Railway is Barrie Sanford, *McCulloch's Wonder* (North Vancouver: Whitecap Books, 1978 & 2002). Other very useful sources include Roger Burrows, *Railway Mileposts: British Columbia* (2 vols.; North Vancouver: Railway Milepost Books, 1981, 1984); Gerry Doeksen, *Kettle Valley Railway* (Montrose, BC: Gerry Doeksen, 1995); Beth Hill, *Exploring the Kettle Valley Railway* (Winlaw, BC: Polestar Press, 1989); Barrie Sanford, *Steel Rails and Iron Men; A Pictorial History of the Kettle Valley Railway* (North Vancouver: Whitecap Books, 1990 & 2003); Joe Smuin, *Kettle Valley Railway Mileboards* (Winnipeg: North Kildonan Publications, 2003); and Robert Turner, *Steam on the Kettle Valley* (Victoria: Sono Nis Press, 1995). Other short popular accounts include Anne Mayhew, "Steaming the Kettle," *Beautiful British Columbia* (March 1994); Elizabeth Olson, "The Legend of the KVR," *Western Living* (May 1981).

[2] Quoted in Hill, 10.

[3] Hill, 10-11.

[4] The terms of the agreement stipulated that the KVR acquire the assets and debts of the defunct Midway and Vernon Railway and complete the Midway to Nicola line within four years (and thereby link up with a branch CPR line already at Merritt). The BC government would provide a subsidy of $5,000 per mile for the line between Penticton and Nicola, give the KVR free right-of-way

through crown lands and exempt the railway temporarily from some taxes. There was no mention of the line through the Coquihalla Pass since the KVR had not yet obtained the statutory authority to build it.

[5] Sanford, *McCulloch's Wonder*, 121-122.

[6] Warren remained as KVR president until 1920 when he moved to the Consolidated Mining and Smelting Company (Cominco) as president, a post he held until his death in January 1939.

[7] Andrew McCulloch, "The Railway Development in Southern British Columbia from 1890 On," November 1938, Penticton, BC, Penticton Museum & Archives (PMA).

[8] A surveying crew which wintered in 1915 and 1916 noted the record of 67 feet (21 m). (Sanford, 184)

[9] The defeat of the Wilfred Laurier government in 1911 and the abandonment of the idea of a Canada/US reciprocity agreement which would have benefited the GN and VV&E, changed the political environment.

[10] The Trout Creek bridge had 450 feet of approach trestles (137 m) for the 250 foot steel truss bridge (77 m) which stood 241 feet (73 m) above the creek.

[11] Joe Smuin, author of *Kettle Valley Railway Mileboards,* questions whether the Quintette Tunnels were McCulloch's idea alone. The Great Northern/VV&E survey which predates that of the KVR shows a very similar alignment. (Smuin to author, February 29, 2008.)

[12] Andrew McCulloch diary, September 28, 1911, PMA.

CHAPTER II

PREPARATIONS: MYRA CANYON AND WESTWARD

Trains travelling west from Midway encountered the first of the spectacular vistas on the KVR section just above Kelowna. They clattered over magnificent bridges, accessed dramatic panoramas of the valley below and drew near to superb fishing and hunting opportunities. Further down the line they passed through an unusual horseshoe-shaped tunnel. This is the segment that began at Hydraulic Lake, click-clacked around Myra Canyon, ran above a daunting gorge at Sawmill Creek (Bellevue Creek), continued on a gentle grade to Chute Lake, negotiated loops at both Adra and Glenfir and then dropped down into the valley, skirting Naramata before arrival at lake level in Penticton. It was a magnificent run promoted in the tourist brochures as the gateway to the Okanagan Valley. Moreover, it was a challenging route as it contained the high spot of the KVR followed by one of its low points. It incorporated an elevation drop of nearly 3,000 feet, from 4,133 feet above sea level in Myra Canyon to 1,145 feet in Penticton.[1] The challenge of the run signified another ordeal: the struggle to build the line. To plan, supply, man and construct this segment tested the skills and resources of its creators and the endurance of its workers.

Why did the KVR pass over this particular route, especially when there were other possibilities further south and north? When McCulloch was appointed Chief Engineer, Thomas Shaughnessy stipulated a number of conditions for the railway's routing. The most relevant condition affecting our story was that the line must travel from Midway to Carmi.[2] This requirement meant that a line via Hydraulic Lake was seen as the best option for the KVR to cross the highlands between the Kettle River watershed and the Okanagan Valley.[3]

At first it was thought that the route would be fairly straightforward. As originally surveyed in 1911 by McCulloch's deputy, William Gourlay, the route planned a generally uniform descending grade not exceeding 1.5 per cent from Hydraulic Lake to Penticton. This route meant passing through Myra Canyon, on

Surveyor William Gourlay and an associate. Gourlay conducted the original Midway to Penticton survey from early 1911 to 1912. McCulloch later changed the route from Myra Canyon and re-worked the line through the Chute Lake pass to include the well known loops at Adra and Glenfir.

Penticton Museum

to Sawmill Creek, past Cedar Creek, around the west face of Okanagan Mountain close to the lake and Squally Point and finally down to Penticton. But when McCulloch examined this plan closely and compared it to his observations of the terrain, he recognized several major problems. The first issue for him involved Myra Canyon and its cousin, the chasm at Sawmill Creek.

Myra Canyon, generally known as Five Fingers Canyon, appeared in the shape of a rough "W" as it dipped into the east and west forks of Canyon Creek, today's KLO and Pooley Creeks. Occasionally it was called Canyon Creek or Cañon Creek or KLO Creek Canyon (after the Kelowna Land & Orchard Company). Only in the 1980's did people begin using the term Myra Canyon widely, adopting the name of the nearest station to the east. This designation honoured Myra Newman, the daughter of a tracklaying foreman.[4]

McCulloch's writings do not dwell on the difficulties of negotiating Myra Canyon, although he was not particularly flattering in his comments. The first time he saw it in November 1910, he wrote: "Got a team and drove out to look for

KVR surveyors packing up to move camp. Horses could manage loads up to 270 pounds if they were evenly distributed. The box standing on its side is labelled St. Charles Milk (condensed), a staple in the construction camps. *Penticton Museum*

An early stage of surveying near Myra Canyon. The surveyors have cut a six foot working swath in order to establish a precise location for the line. The man in the foreground is using an inclinometer and is making notations in his notebook. His companion is carrying a transit level.

Penticton Museum

Gourlay.... Out along the line.... Back to Canon Creek.... Damn bad canyon there. Will be five or six miles of villainously heavy work. Whole hillside is bad enough.... Canon Creek district all rock." A year's contemplation did not change that view. In September 1911, he noted: "Hell of a climb.... Gourlay has a bad country. Canon Creek and Sawmill Creek are bad."[5] Nor did this view change by 1912. Two entries in his diary that next year reflected his uncomplimentary opinion of Myra. In June he opined: "Climbed up along Canon Ck. Up to elevation 4550 and then up and down along by the forks of the creek. Bad place. Any amount of ups and downs." He followed in September with another lament: "Looked around the canon and all around.... Hell of a country up here."[6]

He was right; it was a hell of a country. The first problem with Myra Canyon surfaced when McCulloch carefully examined Gourlay's proposed route and

After the surveyors had established the route, the KVR contracted with clearing gangs to cut down and remove the trees from the path. This photograph, probably taken in 1912 somewhere near Myra Canyon, includes left to right: Alec Larson, Pete Anderson, Fred Falk, Gust Stattingren and H. Westerland on the rock. The tent features a wooden floor, an external wood frame and stove pipe. Pete has his axe and gloves while Fred holds a rifle. These gangs augmented their diet by hunting game. *Penticton Museum*

compared it to his read of the topography. The preliminary survey had the line passing through Myra Canyon at a lower point than was eventually built, to achieve the 1.5 per cent grade. The lower line, however, meant a very expensive crossing of Sawmill Creek and its canyon further down. The chasm there was very wide with very steep walls. That route had some advantages, nevertheless, a key one being that it brought the line closer to Kelowna which would have served the population of the Central Okanagan. But since the initial route entailed considerable time and expense and the difficulties could be offset with a viable alternative, McCulloch decided to use a higher elevation in both canyons.[7] This decision did not make the citizens of Kelowna very happy. When the first hint of a possible change filtered down to that community, the local newspaper complained: "A higher elevation … will mean that the line will be entirely out of reach so far as the passenger and freight business of this district is concerned."[8] Some time later when work on the grade itself was visible, another paper continued the grumble: "To the residents of Kelowna … it seems that a very long time will elapse before they can see the rails coming toward the city, instead of going away from the district, as at present."[9] Nonetheless, McCulloch's expediency and practicality took precedence.

A survey crew and their equipment defining the route adjacent to a rock face. The men, working on the line, possibly through Myra Canyon, had difficult terrain to negotiate and survey. A primitive log hut with a chimney is located in the lower left corner. *Northwest Museum of Arts & Culture, Spokane, Washington*

Canyon depths were not the only surveying concern between Myra and Penticton. McCulloch noted that Gourlay's plan with the 1.5 per cent grade pushed the line around the outside of the mountain ridge just east of Okanagan Lake and involved numerous tunnels and bridges. It also necessitated a large number of tight curves which jeopardized the operating advantage of the moderate grade. As with the two canyons McCulloch had an alternative: stay level after Sawmill Creek and then cut through a narrow pass just south of Chute Lake. Although this option was easy for much of the way, it did mean the route emerged only 15 miles from Penticton while still nearly 3,000 feet above the lake. This is when McCulloch realized that to connect the pass with the city, he required grades of up to 4.5 per cent, grades which bordered on the impossible.

McCulloch began seriously to address this problem in late May 1912. For the next several months he examined, calculated and considered what to do. He recognized that going via Chute Lake pass would still not avoid the heavy work through Myra Canyon but the run from there to the pass was essentially level and involved much easier construction than Gourlay's route around the mountain edge. But, what could he do once he emerged from the pass? It was here that he hit upon his bold idea of a steady 2.2 per cent grade out of Penticton and a line which doubled back on itself twice and passed through a curved tunnel before arriving just below Chute Lake. Although the 2.2 per cent grade exceeded the original 1.5 per cent plan, McCulloch calculated that the increase would be offset by fewer curves and noticeably lower construction costs. In fact, when the survey was done and the cost estimates calculated, McCulloch was spot on.[10]

Meanwhile, in August 1912 Warren and McCulloch let the contract for the grading and the construction of the trestles on the 58.2 miles from Hydraulic Summit to Penticton to Grant Smith & Company. This outfit, headquartered in St. Paul, Minnesota, had submitted the lowest bid and had considerable experience building Canadian railways. It also had an important partnership with a Vancouver firm headed by Angus McDonnell. The contract was substantial at more than two million dollars. Of considerable importance to local businesses was the announcement that it would take about two and a-half years to complete, very welcome economic news indeed.

What followed immediately was a flurry of activity and considerable anticipation by local merchants up and down the Okanagan valley. From Penticton came the exclamation: "The terms of the contract require work to be started at once from Penticton and all the material for the line is to be freighted through the town. Consequently, Penticton merchants are well pleased with the outlook

Grant Smith and Company had the general contract for the grade between Hydraulic Summit and Penticton. It rented warehouse facilities on Water Street in Kelowna and built a general office in Naramata. Pay hours there, as seen in this picture, were between 11 am and 12 noon and 3 and 4 pm. Although navvies were paid once each month, many of the labourers quit between pay periods. Those who quit were issued a pay cheque which they then had to take to the office to cash.   *Penticton Museum*

for the next six months."[11] The citizens of Naramata, a bit further north, saw similar prospects and opportunity: "Naramata is to be the base of supplies and the headquarters of the contractors for railway construction work on the east side of the Lake."[12] Further along, Okanagan Mission prepared for the same wave of prosperity, although the paper there announced it with a slightly different twist. The Mission would share in "entertaining the 'railroad men' after pay day."[13] Kelowna residents probably had the greatest expectations or at least, the *Orchard City Record* presented a very optimistic view of the next months:

> *A development of the utmost importance to Kelowna has arisen this week in the renting by Messrs. Smith & Grant ... of the old cannery on Water Street for the purpose of offices and warehouse.... Kelowna will be the principal centre from which the work will be directed and it is here that the men amounting to between 2,000 and 3,000 will be engaged and paid. Fully 70 per cent of the business, we are assured, will be handled in Kelowna, the rest at points down the lake.[14]*

Those living at the "points down the lake" may have disagreed as to who benefited the most, but they all clearly supported the reporter for the *Kelowna Courier*: "It is easy to see that the merchants of the eastern towns on the lake will do some business while the labourers are drilling and blasting."[15]

CARMI SUBDIVISION

Midway to Penticton
(1914 - 1978)

Hwy 97 → Rutland

Hwy 97 to Penticton

KELOWNA Hwy 33

Okanagan Mission

Myra Road

McCulloch Road

Hwy 33

MYRA

RUTH

McCULLOCH

Myra Canyon

McCulloch (Hydraulic) Lake

LORNA

COOKSON

CHUTE LAKE

X
Little White Mtn.
7122 ft.
2170 m.

GLENFIR

ADRA

NARAMATA

LAKEVALE

West Fork Kettle River

Hwy 97 to Kelowna

ARAWANA

Wilkinson Creek Loop

LOIS

PENTICTON 1914 - 1941

POPLAR GROVE

SAWYER

CARMI → **CARMI**

PENTICTON

OSOYOOS SUBDIVISION
Penticton to Osoyoos

SOUTH PENTICTON 1914 - 1941
PENTICTON 1941 - 1989

BEAVERDELL → **BEAVERDELL**

Hwy 97 →

DELLWYE

To Osoyoos or Vancouver

Site of Peanut Point Water Tank

Approximate site of Peanut Point, pioneer landmark on Beaverdell - Westbridge wagon road.

TAURUS

KVR Bull Creek Canyon locally known as: "The Falls" or "Rhone Canyon."

Hwy 33

Christian Valley Road

RHONE

Kettle River

X
Mt. Baldy
7558 ft.
2303 m.

WESTBRIDGE → **WESTBRIDGE**

ZAMORA

Hwy 33

ROCK CREEK
KETTLE VALLEY

Hwy 3 to Osoyoos

Hwy 3

WEST MIDW
MIDWAY WY
MIDWAY
MIDWA

Hwy 3 to Grand For

ROCK CREEK

Kettle River

CANADA

UNITED STATES

Approx. 5 miles

Approx. 5 kms

THE GRANT SMITH CONTRACT

J. J. Warren to Thomas Shaughnessy, Penticton, August 10, 1912

re Line from Penticton to Kettle Okanagan Summit. I have let the contract for this work to Messrs Grant Smith & Company, on the following prices:

Solid Rock	94¢ per cubic yard
Loose Rock	40¢ per cubic yard
Hardpan	34¢ per cubic yard
Earth	18¢ per cubic yard
Tunnel Solid Rock	60.00 per lineal foot
Tunnel Solid Rock outside cross section	3.50 per cubic yard
Tunnel Loose Material	50.00 per lineal foot
Tunnel Loose Material outside cross section	2.75 per cubic yard
Other prices in proportion	

I got tenders from Foley, Welsh & Stewart, Twohey Bros. and Palmer Bros. & Henning as well as Grant Smith & Co: the latter were the lowest tenderers. The work is to be completed by the 1st July 1913.

While the revision of the Gourlay line is not yet finished, the contractors are getting in their camps during the next month, by the expiration of which we will be ready to have the work proceed. There is a good deal of rock in this section of the line and the work can therefore be as well prosecuted in winter as in summer.

Canadian Pacific Archives, Montreal

As rapidly as possible, subcontracts were let, gangs of navvies organized and the preliminary work undertaken. Subletting the various contracts was fairly straightforward and was standard practice among railway firms. The 1914 Royal Commission on Labour in BC spelled it out quite clearly:

The rule in practice appears to be for a firm of contractors to secure the contract for a very extensive mileage, upon which they may or may not do any work themselves, but most of which is sublet by them at a clear profit to some other firm, which may be a branch of the main firm, who in turn sublet to someone else, not without profit naturally, who again sublet to station-men, who do the actual work and receive the smallest profit of all.[16]

In some cases this process involved four levels of subcontractors.

Maybe it was standard practice but subletting led to other problems associated with price gouging. The original contractor furnished all the supplies to his first subcontractor for a profit of 10 per cent. This man in turn supplied goods to the next lower subcontractor for another 10 per cent markup and he did likewise for those subcontractors beneath him. Each took a profit of at least 10 per cent until arriving at the final level, the man with the shovel, who then had to pay excessive prices for what he needed. Consequently, as with so many large projects of this era, those at the top benefited, those just below profited and those in the middle gained, but as we shall see there were few rewards for the navvy doing the real work.[17]

In the case of Grant Smith, while the company reserved some five miles of actual work for itself, it sublet to 12 other firms and these in turn frequently sublet to others. Two of the 12, George Chew of Spokane and E. A. Morrissey, staked out Myra Canyon for grading and building trestles. Chew eventually established 12 camps stretching from Hydraulic Summit (mile 0) over both forks of Canyon Creek to mile 12. Morrissey for his part worked the remaining grade and undertook the trestle construction from mile 12 to 16. His men laboured from two camps, both located near the future Ruth Station in Myra Canyon. The other subcontractors down the line included Swan Benson, Kimball Brothers & Campbell, King Walsh, Davenport Gray & Company, Gilbert Brandt, Bacher Harmount & Company, Griffin Hunt, the Valley Construction Company, the Schacht Brothers and the Schacht Company of Carroll Street, Vancouver, as well as Grant Smith's own camps. Of the nearly $2.5 million that Grant Smith paid out to his subcontractors, George Chew clearly had the largest operation as he received the most money at over $500,000. Morrissey's share for his work in Myra was nearly $190,000, the sixth largest amount paid out.[18]

Specialized sub-subcontractors also played an important role. In Myra Canyon a firm named Huissi engaged mainly in trestle construction while another, Anderson, undertook tunnel building. Further towards Penticton, others took on various unspecified tasks: Dibble (near Sawmill Creek), Blair (at Chute Lake), Alexander (near the tunnel at mile 38) and Shott (three miles from Naramata). There were undoubtedly others but those names have not yet surfaced.

For the first few weeks the contractors busied themselves preparing for the work, bringing in quantities of supplies, hiring scores of navvies, building miles of tote or service roads and establishing work camps. Some idea of the activities, quantities and methods employed was provided by the *Penticton Herald:* "Camp material was shipped down the lake … last Monday. Fourteen heavy drays loaded

Subcontractor Gilbert Brandt's Camp #2 above Naramata. This camp utilized both tent and log construction. The tents had a partial wooden wall, a wooden door and a canvas top. Each one had a stove. The log houses were made from rough timber. The ends of the logs have not been evenly cut nor have the logs been chinked which imply a temporary camp. Each log house has several vents on the roof for air circulation inside. A wood pile is on the right. *Penticton Museum*

with tents, stoves, beds and all the necessaries for the comfort of the men were loaded on No. 2 scow.... The whole were towed by the steamer Aberdeen."[19] Meanwhile, gangs of men arrived daily and went to work as fast as possible – 50 navvies to unload, another 200 to build camps and 300 more to construct the roads. The evidence of their labour was everywhere, but the most important evidence was the 65 miles of wagon roads they soon built. McCulloch called them "good, bad and indifferent," but they were crucial. He himself emphasized that point: "As the line is on hillside all the way and the country is very rough, the making of roads and getting in of supplies are big undertakings."[20] George Chew and E. A. Morrissey in Myra Canyon had probably the longest and toughest haul. Not only did the trip to their camps entail a three-day round trip from Kelowna, the supplies had to move from lake level at 1,125 feet to heights of 4,000 feet.[21]

While the contractors busied themselves so did the railway. In order to oversee the work in a systematic and continuous manner, the KVR needed camps for its own personnel. A quick note on the KVR's engineering hierarchy will clarify how this worked. McCulloch as Chief Engineer directed a number of Assistant Engineers, each in charge of several sections of construction, location parties or

Freighting on the K.V. Ry.
W.chler

This four horse team hauled supplies along one of the 65 miles of tote roads built to provision the construction camps between Hydraulic Summit and Naramata. Goods were carried for a penny a pound. There is not much slash scattered around which means the photo was probably taken after July 1913. In that month the fire warden directed the KVR to burn all piles of slash along the tote roads as they presented a major fire hazard.

Northwest Museum of Arts & Culture, Spokane, Washington

other important work. On the Hydraulic to Penticton section he had two Assistant Engineers, G. W. Buck, who dealt with miles 0 to 28 (which included Myra Canyon) and M. E. Brooks, responsible for miles 28 to 58. They in turn had several Resident Engineers, in direct charge of shorter sections, who reported to them.[22] All these engineers and their staff (clerks, time keepers, surveying crews and payroll personnel) required housing. One of the first engineers' camps was established south of Three Mile Point between Penticton and Naramata in September 1912.[23] The others were scattered along the line at appropriate intervals.

It was not just the contractors and the railway folks who were busy with preparations. The local citizens launched their various enterprises and joined in the boom. In September 1912 a company began a stage service between Kelowna and Carmi. Such a venture held great promise as noted by the local paper. Others, observing the many men passing through Kelowna, addressed their needs. One

NOT EVERYONE WAS HAPPY ABOUT THE NAVVIES

There is urgent necessity of a sufficient force of constables to prevent so much thieving. It seems an impossibility with the present force to prevent the thieving propensities of many of the large number of foreigners now arriving here and it is high time they were taught what British customs are. We want a lot of extra men who will control such individuals.

W. D. McKie to the Editor, *Kelowna Courier,* November 21, 1912

enterprising individual remodelled his house near the downtown, converting it into a spacious bunkhouse to relieve the congestion in the city hotels. Meanwhile, in the Okanagan Mission the revamped Bellevue Hotel profited from its location near the wharf where supplies and men landed for the camps. Many of the workers and some of the freighters stayed there on their way to the grade. Any number of local businesses thus profited, not just in Kelowna but Naramata and Penticton as well as Summerland across the lake.[24]

Great expectations clearly were evident on the east side of Okanagan Lake that late summer of 1912. The railway had really arrived: it had completed its surveys, engaged good contractors, hired navvies, kindled economic activity and laid down its roots. More than a whiff of optimism was in the air; there was the promise of great achievements. First, of course, contractors had grades to level, tunnels to drill and blast and trestles to build, but these were the basics of construction. They would present no great difficulties – or would they?

---

[1] I decided to use only feet and miles from this point forward since those were the measurements employed during the KVR construction era. A conversion chart for metric, however, is found on the last page of the index.

[2] This requirement was likely because the KVR had acquired the charter and subsidies of the defunct Midway to Vernon railway.

[3] Barrie Sanford provided invaluable information for a number of the details in this chapter. (Various correspondence with the author, especially July 2, 2007.)

[4] "Myra" was one of three "daughter" stations. Ruth McCulloch and Lorna Warren were the origins for the other two.

[5] McCulloch diary, September 29, 1910 & September 28, 1911, PMA.

[6] McCulloch diary, June 6, 1912 & September 21, 1912, Barrie Sanford Archives (BSA).

[7] Warren commented on this change: "The crossing of Saw Mill Creek on this first

line was in a canyon 400 feet deep and 600 ft. across, several miles in length, with precipitous walls. The crossing on the second line will not be more than 100 ft long and there is no canyon." (Warren to Shaughnessy, Memo 19, June 5, 1911, CP Archives, Montreal [CPA].)

8 "Local and Personal News," *Kelowna Courier and Okanagan Orchardist*, May 18, 1911, 5.

9 "Kelowna," *Vernon News,* January 22, 1914, 8.

10 Sanford, 142-143. See also Andrew McCulloch field diary, 1912 (photocopy available Penticton Museum).

11 "News of the Province," *Kelowna Courier,* August 8, 1912, 4.

12 "Naramata Head-Quarters for Railway Work," *Summerland Review,* August 16, 1912, 1.

13 "Our Neighbours," *Kelowna Courier,* September 19, 1912, 2.

14 "Kettle Valley Contractors Make Headquarters Here," *Orchard City Record* (Kelowna), September 12, 1912, 1.

15 "Our Neighbours."

16 British Columbia Commission on Labour 1912-1914, British Columbia Archives (BCA), Victoria.

17 *Report of the BC Commission on Labour*, March, 1914. The report recommended legislation that would prevent granting large contracts to firms unless they undertook all the work themselves. It also continued: "The commission finds that the system of sub-contracting on the railroad work is injurious to the interests of the labourer. The custom of sub-letting construction, as many as four sub-contracts in some instances being made, is one that should be restricted. If the government should require contractors to do the actual work of construction the commission believes that the labourer would secure a better wage and better living conditions."

18 An audit of Grant Smith's books, as part of a lawsuit against the KVR, reveals the various payments to the subcontractors:

George Chew	$543,356.36
Gilbert Brandt & Company	386,515.07
Grant Smith & Company's camps	211,806.67
Bacher Harmount & Company	203,547.67
Swan Benson & Company	202,509.54
E. A. Morrissey & Company	189,085.55
Kimball Bros. & Campbell	185,704.21
Valley Construction Company	141,271.03
Davenport Gray & Company	132,786.12
King Walsh & Company	106,964.30
Griffin Hunt & Company	106,623.10
Schacht Bros	68,124.40
Schacht Company	57,562.13
Total	$2,535,856.15

Edwards, Morgan & Company, Chartered Accountants, to Kettle Valley Railway, Vancouver, February 3, 1917, BSA.

[19] "Start Made on Ten Mile Grade," *Penticton Herald,* September 21, 1912, 1.

[20] Andrew McCulloch, *Annual Report,* 1912, Midway to Merritt, BSA.

[21] There were three access roads from Kelowna which came off what is now McCulloch Road. The two other main access routes to the grade were from Naramata, for those camps nearer the end of the line, and from Okanagan Mission for the middle section of camps.

[22] The resident engineers were:

Miles 1 – 8	H. W. Gahan
Miles 8 – 13	N. J. McLean
Miles 13 – 21	G. G. Gladman
Miles 22 – 28	A. R. Moore
Miles 28 – 36	N. A. Penticost
Miles 36 – 42	R. L. Alexander
Miles 42 – 49	W. H. Prowse
Miles 49 – 58	C. Q. Bay

Assistant and Resident engineer's reports, KVR, PMA.

The mileage indication began at Mile 0, Hydraulic Summit. The summit itself was Mile 76.05 from Midway. It was unclear who had responsibility for Mile 21-22.

[23] "Kettle Valley Railway," *Vernon News,* September 26, 1912, 1.

[24] "Local and Personal News," *Kelowna Courier,* September 26, 1912, 5; "Local and Personal News," *Kelowna Courier,* October 17, 1912, 5.

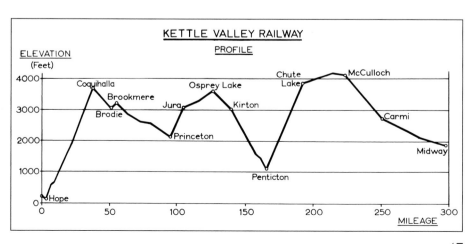

1913 MAP
Includes mileage from Hydraulic Summit

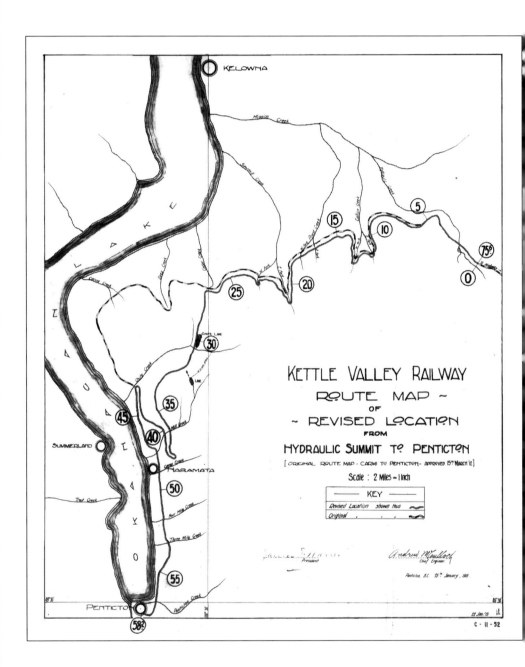

CHAPTER III

INTO HIGH GEAR

The heavy work of scraping and levelling, digging, drilling and blasting, along with sawing and hammering began easily enough in late September 1912. Starting first out of Penticton, the navvies and their bosses tackled the grade with considerable gusto, a move which brought obvious satisfaction to J. J. Warren. The KVR president had not been overly impressed with the contractors working on the line elsewhere, but now he offered praise for his latest selection: "Grant Smith & Co. ... seem to be taking hold of the work better than any contractors have taken hold of any other section."[1] This launch in the south was quickly extended and soon there was great activity coming on the Hydraulic end as well. Navvies picked and scraped, horses hauled and dumped and the grade moved forward. The progress here brought a proud announcement by one of Kelowna's newspapers: "The Kettle Valley grade on the hill to the southeast is now quite visible from town and the blasting operations can be seen and heard any morning."[2] As the pace intensified the work force expanded. By year's end 880 men and 56 teams laboured, continuing as Warren wrote, "to make good progress with this section."[3] These numbers would grow to a peak exceeding 2,000 men in 1913.

As with any construction project, the unexpected occurred. First, it was the rock. The KVR engineers knew they had extensive rock cuts ahead of them but no one anticipated that the rock would be quite so hard. As McCulloch described it: "The rock especially on the lower end miles 27 to 53 [near Sawmill Creek to past Naramata] turned out to be very hard and from a contractors point of view, poor rock to handle."[4] At first the contractors bemoaned it. Later their complaints turned into lawsuits. Their litigation focused initially on the change of route, but the extensive, hard rock played its part as well.

Another problem involved several land owners between Penticton and Naramata who were unwilling to accept the KVR's offer for their land and a right-of-way. This brought the work of grading that section to a standstill for nearly eight

Myra Canyon

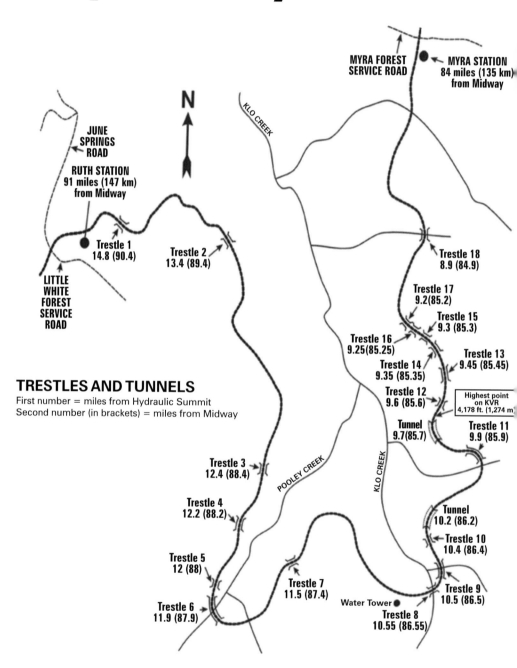

MYRA FOREST
SERVICE ROAD

MYRA STATION
84 miles (135 km)
from Midway

KLO CREEK

N

JUNE
SPRINGS
ROAD

RUTH STATION
91 miles (147 km)
from Midway

Trestle 1
14.8 (90.4)

Trestle 2
13.4 (89.4)

Trestle 18
8.9 (84.9)

LITTLE
WHITE
FOREST
SERVICE
ROAD

Trestle 17
9.2(85.2)

Trestle 15
9.3 (85.3)

Trestle 16
9.25(85.25)

Trestle 13
9.45 (85.45)

Trestle 14
9.35 (85.35)

TRESTLES AND TUNNELS
First number = miles from Hydraulic Summit
Second number (in brackets) = miles from Midway

Trestle 12
9.6 (85.6)

Highest point
on KVR
4,178 ft. (1,274 m)

Tunnel
9.7(85.7)

Trestle 11
9.9 (85.9)

Trestle 3
12.4 (88.4)

POOLEY CREEK

KLO CREEK

Trestle 4
12.2 (88.2)

Tunnel
10.2 (86.2)

Trestle 10
10.4 (86.4)

Trestle 5
12 (88)

Trestle 7
11.5 (87.4)

Trestle 9
10.5 (86.5)

Trestle 6
11.9 (87.9)

Water Tower

Trestle 8
10.55 (86.55)

Drilling Machine in Tunnel,

The rock in Adra Tunnel near Naramata proved to be very hard, making it extremely slow going for the manual drilling crew. This drill machine was brought in to speed up the work. Once the operator positioned the heavy tripod and connected the air compression hose, he began work. The tripod remained stationary while the drill moved forward as it penetrated the rock. *Penticton Museum*

months after January 1913. It became such a serious issue that the contractor, C. R. Schacht, cancelled his contract, pointing out that it was too costly for him to remain idle. He discharged nearly 70 men and pulled out 30 teams of horses as well as his camp equipment. Only after the KVR went to the courts and persuaded a judge to enforce the expropriation did work resume in late September. Schacht then returned.[5]

Contractors also faced manpower problems. A shortage of labour was not unusual. On any railway project there were always three groups of workers – those coming, those going and those working. As explained by a reporter from Penticton: "You may have a full gang today, tomorrow they go down to town and the next day another gang arrives – and so it goes on."[6] But contractors on the KVR faced a chronic labour shortage which dogged them through 1913 and 1914. Both Warren and McCulloch made frequent references to the problem. Warren wrote in May 1913: "It seems difficult to keep men on this section [Hydraulic to Penticton] or any other section of work for that matter in British Columbia. They keep coming and going all the time and quit on the slightest provocation."[7] McCulloch added, no less concerned: "The labor conditions were not very good; men were hard to get."[8]

In Myra Canyon the subcontractor, E. A. Morrissey, seemingly had the most difficult time obtaining and keeping men; sometimes he found they left the same day that they arrived. In July 1913 McCulloch reported that everything was progressing well, "except on sub-contractor Morissey's [sic] work where 45 men quit and left the job." A few weeks later another engineer wrote: "Morrissey's force is too small. He claims he is trying everywhere to get more men and needs 100 to 125." Then, in September it was: "Morrissey still dragging along unable to get more men," a lament which continued into the new year 1914 and reoccurred regularly until his contract ended. One might begin to suspect, however, that there was more here than manpower issues. Assistant Engineer Buck once reported: "Work progressing satisfactorily except Morrissy [sic], who is inclined to shirk and hold back." Other contractors suffered similar problems but Morrissey of Myra Canyon figured prominently in any mention of labour scarcities.[9]

In the end most contractors obtained the men they needed, but they faced another problem. Talk of a strike loomed over the KVR's labour pool late in 1912 and into the spring of 1913. BC was already alive with strike fever as a result of the navvies' walkout against the Canadian Northern in March, April and May 1912.[10] That fever had filtered south. Even before Warren had awarded the contract to Grant Smith, reports of union activity surfaced in the Penticton area. As soon as the subcontractors established their camps, the organizers and

Six men and a horse posing for the photographer near Myra Canyon. The rail cart and the temporary track were used for hauling the rock from the cut behind the men to the next low spot. *Penticton Museum*

The handwritten caption on the reverse of this photograph reads: "Working on the Grade, K. V. Ry., Grant Smith & Co., 1913." *Penticton Museum*

champions of the International Workers of the World (IWW or the Wobblies), the famous American-based syndicalist union, moved in and attempted to organize the men. Many of the workers, the so-called stiffs,[11] welcomed them, but not so the contractors and the authorities. At one camp the IWW organizers faced the hostility of the contractor's family who clubbed them. At another the foreman telephoned the authorities for help. At a third site the police arrived and arrested the IWW men. Usually the enforcers of the law incarcerated the organizers and not infrequently marched them out of the region. If the men appeared in court, judges moved quickly to fine or sentence them to hard labour. The stiffs may have supported and valued the IWW but the welcome certainly stopped there. The union had no other support.[12]

Resistance to the Wobblies, however, did not hinder them; work stoppages began anyway. In late March 1913 most of the men at Gilbert Brandt's camp, near Naramata, struck for a pay increase from $2.75 to $3 per day. In April about 100 men quit, owing to the discharge of an IWW man. Then on May 3 a major disruption commenced with several hundred men walking off their jobs, on strike for better wages and better conditions. Although their action encompassed most of Grant Smith's contract area, including Myra Canyon, the strike centred around

THE IWW AS DEFINED BY JOHN J. O'CONNOR, UNION ORGANIZER

Q. Mr. Mackelvie. What Union is this you mentioned?

A. The Industrial Workers of the World. Headquarters at Chicago.

Q. Mr. Mackelvie. What is the fundamental object of the organization?

A. The fundamental object is to better the conditions of the proletariat, the working classes. In order to better conditions they take any methods that are feasible, as for instance a strike if they think a walk out is the best method. If they think it is best to stay on the job they stay as long as they can and put their demands up to the contractors.

Q. We have been told sometimes that its fundamental principle is destruction? To keep stirring up strife amongst laborers.

A. Oh, it's revolutionary, yes. Incidentally they do reform but the object, in short terms, is industrial socialism.... We have organized on the principle that an injury to one is an injury to all and that if you are thoroughly organized you can take some action. So of course it's a revolutionary proposition to change conditions.

BC Commission on Labour, May 6, 1913, Penticton

the tunnel camps out of Naramata. Some reports said as many as 1,000 men went out, although that number probably included those who quit and moved on, not just the active participants. The strike began as a noble idea, but lasted only a few days. Enthusiasm quickly faded and the men returned to the camps under the prevailing conditions.[13]

Other factors also affected the labour pool. This time the winds of war intervened. As early as November 1912, some Greek and Balkan itinerants began departing to fight for their countries in the first of the Balkan wars. It was the Great War of August 1914, however, which caused the most disruption. When it first broke out, KVR officials acted with considerable uncertainty, ordering a suspension of work on part of the line east of Princeton. Although all construction quickly resumed, not everyone stayed. Some subjects of the Austro-Hungarian Empire slipped across the US border en route home to support their cause while patriotic British subjects left to enlist for king and country. Before long it became a race to finish the Midway to Penticton section against disappearing manpower and dwindling resources.[14]

Yet despite the problems, the work progressed. Aside from levelling and preparing the grade, the major task requiring attention concerned the tunnels. Initially, McCulloch planned five of them, three in Myra Canyon and two closer to Naramata. One of the three in Myra, however, eventually became a rock cut when McCulloch determined it was too unstable and decided to cut out the top.[15]

The navvies began to drill early in 1913. George Chew had responsibility for the three tunnels in Myra while Bacher Harmount & Company undertook the long one above Naramata and probably the smaller tunnel further down the line. It was slow work, especially as it took a three-man crew drilling an entire day to manage about five feet. George Chew had the easier time of it. He did not have to contend with a major curve in the middle of his work like his colleagues further south nor did he have such distances to bore. He completed his tunnels in mid-July and early August although he often had to put on double shifts to meet his deadlines.[16]

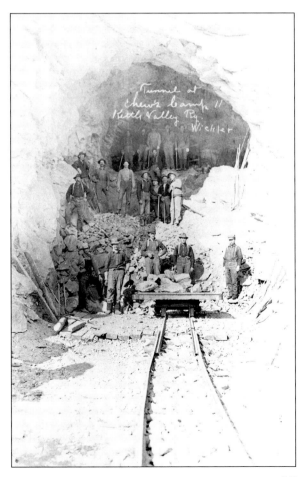

These navvies, employed by subcontractor George Chew, are working on the west tunnel in Myra Canyon (mile 86.2). They are cutting out the tunnel in stages at three levels and they are using a cart which has no sides. Most men hold an eight pound sledge hammer while a number of pry bars for loosening the rock are leaning against the side.

Northwest Museum of Arts & Culture, Spokane, Washington

55

The big tunnel at mile 38 was a significant challenge. The rock there proved very hard and particularly difficult to work. After some weeks and despite double shifts, the contractor had proceeded only a short distance of the required 1,600 feet. To speed up the operation the company brought in a steam drill, intending to replace much of the hand drilling. Even then it was slow-going and hazardous. Numerous accidents attested to the dangers. Not until April 12, 1914, nearly 16 months after commencement, did the tunnelling crews meet midway in what became known as Adra Tunnel. Then the celebrations commenced. Overcoming that major hurdle meant the line could move along more rapidly.[17]

Two men starting to bore a tunnel, probably Adra, January 1913. The man on the left with heavy gloves will hold the nearby metal drill while the other man strikes it.

Penticton Museum

As with any large project, work commenced on several fronts at the same time. In December 1913 Warren announced that his stiffs had finished the grading from Hydraulic to Penticton, except for a few cuts and the tunnel at Adra. Since the railhead had reached Hydraulic Summit and his crews had assembled the first two trestles at miles 1 and 2, the actual job of laying steel could begin, moving in two directions, west from Hydraulic and east from Penticton. For this task the KVR, not the contractors, undertook the work, hiring a crew of about 100 men.[18]

The effort was exciting, both in the real work and what it represented. Midway and Penticton were moving closer together. The local papers heralded the announcement and offered this description:

> It is a revelation to the uninitiated ... to see the big tracklaying machine which the contractors are using, at work. The railway ties are shot through a chute and the rails are laid accurately on top. The men who look after the spiking and bolting of the rails have to be very quick, as the trucks of the tracklaying are generally on the rail a fraction of a second after it is fully secured.[19]

Navvies positioning ties and laying steel. One part of the crew puts the ties on the railbed while other navvies lay the rail. The "strikers' then hammer the spikes to secure the rail and the process continues.

Penticton Museum

By the end of January steel had progressed nine miles east of Penticton and nine miles west of Hydraulic. The excitement of this development in the Okanagan Valley could be seen in the enthusiastic support of a local paper: "The line of the Kettle Valley can be seen from Kelowna and it was very pleasing to see a work train on that part of the railway above Canyon Creek last week for the first time."[20]

Continuing progress with the steel occurred primarily on the western end since crews had the necessary trestles there well under construction. By late March 1914 steel had reached the mouth of the big tunnel, some 20 miles from Penticton. Although there followed a month's wait while navvies finished the tunnel, track-laying resumed in mid-May and reached the west fork of Sawmill Creek, about 36 miles from Penticton by early June. Another wait ensued while crews assembled the two trestles over the west and east forks, but early in September the steel raced on, reaching Myra Canyon and its challenges.[21]

In Myra Canyon, McCulloch's plan called for the navvies to construct 19 wooden trestles allowing the line to skirt the canyon. Seventeen of those trestles still exist today, 12 of which were re-built after the devastating 2003 fire. One trestle at mile 10.9 was covered with fill in 1928 while a revised line in 1946 bypassed another at mile 12.6. Also in 1928 the company built a new trestle at mile 12.4 (trestle 3) to compensate for the gap caused by some hillside slippage. Thus the total number in Myra Canyon today is 18.[22]

It was not especially difficult to build these trestles, but there were so many of them in such a short distance and each one had to be completed before the next one could begin. McCulloch explained the situation in his 1913 annual report: "On account of the trestles being located in rough places and the line being up on hillside, … it was decided to erect the trestles from the end of track, that is, to lay track to the site, haul the timber in by train and erect the trestle."[23]

Generally each one took one to two weeks to erect, although the larger ones like those at the east and west forks of Canyon Creek required up to a month to complete. That the stiffs could put up a trestle in such a short time was because other crews had already prepared the foundations. These other navvies had worked steadily on the foundation pits since August 1913, completing all the groundwork by February 1914. Further, at least 100 carpenters framed each trestle in Carmi (except for today's trestles 1 and 2 which probably came from Naramata). These carpenters had also worked steadily for some months. Using mainly fir shipped from the coast they fashioned the trestles which work trains then hauled to the end of the line.[24]

Two men, a woman and a dog posing, probably on trestle 3 in Myra Canyon (mile 88.4), about 1928.

Barrie Sanford Archives

With everything ready the men started the task of erection and assembly. George Chew's crews put together the trestles between miles 8.9 and 10.55 (today's trestles 18 to 8). E. A. Morrissey constructed those between miles 12 and 14.77 (trestles 5 through 1), although he sub-contracted a part of his work to a builder named Huissi. Just which contractor, Chew or Morrissey, completed trestles 6 and 7 remains unclear.

It was fast work, but it was work that required exact planning by the engineers and amazing skills by the carpenters. McCulloch, like other engineers of his generation, would not allow shims in the trestles (there were only two of them in Myra) so the measurements and pre-fabricated construction required close precision. Chew's crew began the first trestle (today's number 18) on January 6, 1914, and then proceeded at the rate of about one per week until they reached trestle number 11 in mid-March at which point they slowed down while they waited for the carpenters and blacksmiths to catch up with timber and metal work. By the third week of April they had reached the east fork of Canyon Creek. With the completion of each trestle, the tracklaying crews placed the steel to the next point. At times they moved so fast they went through a carload of bolts per day. This consumption generated work for some 75 blacksmiths, working mainly

This picture of the gorge which is now bridged by trestle 4 in Myra Canyon (mile 88.2) gives an idea of the challenges of construction. Men first laboured deep in the gorge to build the foundations, then others ran a cable across the gorge in order to carry the wooden vertical supports (bents) which were then positioned into place on top of the footings. Several stories of bents were necessary in order to bring the trestle surface up to the level for the rail line. The construction camp to the right (see arrow) belonged to a subcontractor named Huissi. *Penticton Museum*

in Carmi. Exactly how many men worked on each trestle remains unclear but Warren's reports give some indications. In August and September 1914, when the only construction was in Myra, the contractors had 75 and 60 men respectively erecting trestles.[25]

The trestles themselves consumed an enormous amount of timber. Two reports provide some idea of the volume. First, Resident Engineer N. J. McLean noted on June 30, 1914, that the plan called for 3,804,264 board feet for all of Myra Canyon. To that date, McLean observed, the crews had placed 442,848 board feet in the trestles of mile 9; 962,192 board feet in mile 10; 316,025 board feet in mile 11; and 400,000 board feet plus 28,560 board feet of native timber in mile 12. In early 1915, McCulloch offered another indication when he said that the segment from Hydraulic to Penticton required some 7,431,000 board feet.[26] The KVR obviously supported a number of lumber mills on the coast and on Vancouver Island.

As the day of completion drew near, Warren notified Shaughnessy of his progress: "During [the] month of September [1914] all the trestles except one at Mile 13.5 were completed. Track was all laid except for 300 ft on this bridge."[27] Then, on October 2, 1914, at trestle 2 (mile 13.5) the last rail went down and

West Fork Canyon Creek trestle (Pooley Creek, mile 87.9) shortly after completion in July 1914. Note the multiple stories of bents and the horizontal and diagonal timber supporting and bracing those bents. The view is from high above the west end on the outside of the curve.

Barrie Sanford Archives

the last spike went in. There was not much celebration at the time, merely an acknowledgement that all was finished between Midway and Penticton. Almost as an understatement, McCulloch remarked in his diary: "At office all day. Track connected through to Midway at last. It took a long time, but we made it at last."[28] Warren, of course, notified the CPR bosses and he also alerted Premier McBride that the steel had met at mile 45 east of Penticton.[29]

Undoubtedly part of the reason there was no great hurrah was that other challenges awaited the KVR navvies further west as they pushed through the Coquihalla region and on to Hope. Also one other important task remained here: ballasting, that is, putting crushed rock between the ties to give the rail-bed stability. Company crews had begun that work from Penticton in February 1914. By May they had completed 18.5 miles. Ballasting west from Hydraulic, however, started much later and had progressed only eight miles by August. But then activity intensified as more men joined the work. Crews reached mile 12 from

PROGRESS REPORT, 1914, HYDRAULIC TO PENTICTON

Andrew McCulloch, December 31,1914

	to Dec 31 1913	to Dec 31 1914
Clearing	767 acres	783 acres
Tunnels	1958 lin ft	2553 lin ft
Timber lining tunnels	467,000 BM [Board Measure]	
Timber in culverts	47,200 lin ft	47,200 lin ft
Timber in trestles	700,000 BM	7,431,000 BM
Iron in trestles & culvers	66,000 lbs	481,500 lbs
Track laid (incl sidings)	7 miles	61 miles
Telegraph line		58 miles
Fencing (single fence)		30 miles
Rails used: West from Hydraulic		
miles 0 to 12	72, 73, & 80 lb relay	
miles 12 to 29	80 lb relay	
miles 29 to 58.2	85 lb new	

Barrie Sanford Achives

Hydraulic and mile 34 coming from Penticton in September. A last big push in October, involving 140 men, completed most of the work by the end of that month. In early December McCulloch happily wrote: "Well, we are rid [of] our ballast gangs. Finished up today and will pay off tomorrow." At the same time other contractors completed the parallel protective fencing and the accompanying telegraph line operated by the company.[30] The track from Midway to Penticton was now really finished.

Not unexpectedly, McCulloch was among the first to ride these rails. His diary entries tell the story, as usual in his forthright no-nonsense manner:

> October 16: Out by train Penticton to Midway. First private car to make the journey.... Made the trip okay.... Midway at 6 pm. Good trip. Nice day at that.
>
> October 17: Leave Midway at 7 am and go westward. Cleared up at Carmi. Not bad day at all. Hydraulic at noon. Rain last night has brought down some rocks in the Canon Creek country. Back to Penticton by 6 pm. Two days lost time, but still I suppose might as well be that way.[31]

A Dominion railway inspector had accompanied McCulloch and given his

View from the west side looking across Myra Canyon, taken shortly after the laying of the rail in September 1914. Trestles 15, 14, 13 and 12 (miles 85.3, 85.35, 85.45 and 85.6) are in the distance across the canyon. In the foreground are the untreated ties, cut on two sides, which hold the steel. They await ballasting, i.e., putting gravel between the ties to stabilize them.

Penticton Museum

approval so the KVR could begin formal operations. Warren quickly announced, however, that because the line west of Penticton awaited completion, there was little point in launching regular service. He put the line "on hold," a move which also postponed celebrations for the time being.

Yet the stiffs and their bosses had done their work, celebration or no celebration. The navvies had helped McCulloch, his engineers and the contractors build a line through a tight canyon, skirt around a second gorge and run level to Chute Lake. They had blasted and tunnelled through 1,600 feet of hard rock, negotiated around two loops and worked on a fairly steep grade which ended at lake level in Penticton. They had assembled some three dozen trestles, half of which were crowded into Myra Canyon, drilled four tunnels and blasted through numerous banks of rock. It was not quite all in a day's work but these accomplishments are the living legacy of the thousands of navvies who laboured on the line. It is time, therefore, to learn more about these stiffs and their life in the construction camps.

[1] Warren to Shaughnessy, Memo 35, November 30, 1912, CPA.

[2] A month later Warren added: "These contractors [Grant Smith] are making much better progress with this work than has been made by contractors on either the Kettle River or Penticton west sections." (Warren to Shaughnessy, Memo 36, December 24, 1912, CPA.)

[3] "Town and Country," *Orchard City Record*, November 21, 1912, 6.

[4] Warren to Shaughnessy, Memo 37, January 16, 1913, CPA.

[5] Andrew McCulloch, *Annual Report*, 1913, BSA.

[6] "Work on the KVR Grade Closed Down," *Penticton Herald*, January 18, 1913, 2; "Deadlock Between KVR and Orchardists," *Penticton Herald*, March 15, 1913, 4; "Trout Creek Bridge Nearly Finished," *Orchard City Record*, October 9, 1913, 7. The claims of the property owners were decided by arbitration which generally decided on figures lower than the KVR offers. ("Finding of Arbitration Board," *Penticton Herald*, December 20, 1913, 1.)

[7] F. G. Tily, "Massive Rock Cuts on Kettle Valley Railway," *Penticton Herald*, January 25, 1913, 1.

[8] Warren to Shaughnessy, Memo 41, May 14, 1913, CPA.

[9] McCulloch, *Annual Report*, 1913.

[10] Andrew McCulloch, Weekly Reports, July 31, 1913 and January 7, 1914; G. W. Buck, Assistant Engineer's Weekly Reports, August 7, 1913, September 7, 1913 and December 7, 1913, all reports in PMA.

[11] In March 1912 the IWW organized a strike against the Canadian Northern on the line between Hope and Kamloops. Some 6,000 navvies struck for improved living conditions. It ended when the BC government came to the aid of the railway by raiding IWW halls and their strike camps, arresting some 200 Wobblies and driving others out of the region. One of the best labour songs, "Where the Fraser River Flows," came out of the strike. (A. Ross McCormack, *The Blanketstiffs* {Montreal: National Film Board, 1974}, 11.)

[12] Stiffs or blanketstiffs was another name used in Canada for the navvies. The term came from the blankets they carried over their shoulders containing their possessions.

[13] "Rough Work in BC," *Industrial Worker* (Spokane), February 20, 1913, 1; "IWW's at Work," *Penticton Herald*, February 15, 1913, 4; "Police Persecution Near Naramata, BC," *Industrial Worker*, March 6, 1913, 1; "Naramata,"*Vernon News*, March 13, 1913, 6.

[14] "Strike of Workers at Construction Camps," *Penticton Herald*, March 29, 1913, 1; "Railway Development," *Canadian Railway and Marine World*, June 1913, 278; "The Labour Situation on the K.R.V.R. Construction," *Kelowna Courier*, May 15, 1913, 1; "Railway Labourers near Penticton," *The Labour Gazette*, June 1913, 1421. Chapter 7 will deal more with the strike.

[15] "Kelowna," *Vernon News*, November 7, 1912, 8; "Kettle Valley Railway," *Summerland Review*, August 28, 1914, 5; "Railway Construction to be Continued," *Summerland Review*, September 4, 1914, 1.

[16] McCulloch field diary, July 12, 1913.

[17] "Local News," *Summerland Review*, January 17, 1913, 4; "Town and Country," *Orchard City Record*, July 10, 1913, 4; G. W. Buck, Assistant Engineer's Weekly Report, August 21, 1913, PMA.

[18] Warren to Shaughnessy, Memo 45, September 12, 1913 and Memo 52, April 14, 1914, CPA; "Local News," *Summerland Review*, April 18, 1913, 6.

[19] McCulloch, Weekly Report (ending December 21, 1912), January 16, 1913, PMA; "Railway Stands Ready to tap Okanagan's Wealth," *Penticton Herald*, December 20, 1913, 1.

[20] "Track Laying on K.V.R.," *Orchard City Record,* January 29, 1914, 9.

[21] "Kelowna," *Vernon News,* January 22, 1914, 8.

[22] McCulloch, Weekly Report (ending March 31, 1914), April 13, 1914; McCulloch field diary, September 18, 1914.

[23] The mileage refers to the distance from Hydraulic Summit, mile 0 which was mile 76.05 from Midway. (See Joe Smuin, *Kettle Valley Railway Mileboards* for mileage from Midway.)

[24] McCulloch, *Annual Report,* 1913.

[25] McCulloch, Weekly Report (ending August 7), August 18, 1913 and Weekly Report (ending February 21), March 4, 1914; "K.V.R. Construction is now near Carmi," *Penticton Herald,* September 6, 1913, 1; Warren to Shaughnessy, Memo 50, February 26, 1914, CPA; McCulloch, *Annual Report,* 1914, BSA; Barrie Sanford to the author, July 7, 2007.

[26] See Appendices for start and completion dates of each trestle. Warren to Shaughnessy, Memo 56, August 17, 1914 and Memo 57, September 15, 1914, both in CPA.

[27] N. J. McLean, Resident Engineer's Report No. 74, in G. W. Buck, Assistant Engineer's Weekly Report, June 30, 1914, PMA; McCulloch, *Annual Report,* 1914.

[28] Warren to Shaughnessy, Memo 58, October 14, 1914, CPA.

[29] McCulloch diary, October 2, 1914, BSA.

[30] The telegram read: Warren to McBride, October 6, 1914: "We connected up the Kettle River and Okanagan Valley on Friday last, the steel meeting at mile 45 east Penticton. We now have almost 225 miles of steel laid, of which 175 miles are continuous from Midway to Osprey Lake, via Penticton. Over 90 per cent of the grading of the entire line is completed. All grading will be finished in another month. At the beginning of winter there will remain only 60 miles of track to be laid next year." ("Railway Development," *Canadian Railway and Marine World,* November 1914, 500.)

[31] McCulloch diary, December 5, 1914, BSA. See also Warren to Shaughnessy, Memo 50, February 26, 1914 and Memo 60, December 16, 1914, CPA.

[32] McCulloch diary, October 16 and 17, 1914, BSA.

CHAPTER IV

"THE MEN WHO MOIL FOR CENTS"
(WITH APOLOGIES TO ROBERT SERVICE)

Railway stories have often focused on the great men with the imagination and bravado to build the lines, the William Van Hornes, the Charles Hayes, the J. J. Hills or more locally with the KVR, the Thomas Shaughnessys, the James Warrens and the Andrew McCullochs. That is as it should be. But too often these achievements have overshadowed the stories of the thousands of labourers who did the difficult work of digging, hauling, filling, carrying, spiking, sweating, hurting and occasionally dying. In the key years after 1907 when Canadians built two transcontinental railways, double-tracked the CPR and established numerous additional lines, including the KVR, railway construction workers numbered between 50,000 and 70,000 men, a significant component of Canada's labour force. It is the story of these men that helped determine Canada's social and economic history and that helped determine the destiny of the Okanagan valley and southern British Columbia. These men are the unsung heroes of the Kettle Valley Railway.

There was, of course, the hierarchy of bosses. They ranged from engineers, assistant engineers, resident engineers, contractors and subcontractors, to surveyors, clerks, accountants, inspectors, walking-bosses, camp foremen and timekeepers. They were the men with greater and lesser responsibilities. They were the ones with the education, the training and the skills needed to develop, plan, oversee and build the KVR. They came from eastern Canada, hired on from the United States or arrived from Europe.

But what about the hundreds and thousands of others? What about those who actually cleared the land, hauled the rock, filled the depressions and levelled the grade? What about the labourers who drilled the tunnels, laid the track and spiked the rails? These men, in the full sense of the word, were the "builders" of the KVR.

They called them navvies, blanketstiffs, stiffs, camp-men or sometimes boomers. Originally navvy was a shortened form of "navigator" and originated with the manual labourers who built the numerous navigation canals in 18th century Britain. They typically worked with shovels, pick axes and wheel barrows. When railway construction superseded canal-building in the first half of the 19th century, the term followed these unskilled workmen. The term blanketstiff or stiff, on the other hand, described itinerant, unskilled workers who jumped from job to job packing their blanket-beds. They cut timber in the forest, harvested wheat on the prairies and provided the brawn for building the railways. The term camp-men, conversely, was the designation used by a contemporary, Edmund Bradwin, who wrote with considerable authority on building Canada's railways in the early 1900's. Finally, boomer, used more after the first World War, denoted those who followed the various construction booms.

Before the twentieth century Canadian railways had relied on Irish navvies and then on Chinese coolies for their labour. But large scale Irish migration had stopped and a new political environment deemed Oriental labour unacceptable just as Canada's economy boomed and required an influx of workers. For a brief time the CPR hired British workers, mainly Welsh, but the company soon found

A group of navvies posing at a construction camp in the fall of 1912, above Naramata, near Adra Tunnel. The men have gathered in front of the cook house with their two cooks. Some have clothes either tattered or worn at the knees and all appear very fit.   *Penticton Museum*

them too vociferous and outspoken and unwilling to accept low wages, basic living arrangements and primitive working conditions. Since they all spoke English, the railway also discovered that they had no problem calling attention to their grievances in the press and elsewhere. The CPR had already concluded that they made poor navvies. According to President Shaughnessy: "It would be a huge mistake to send out any more of these men from Wales, Scotland or England ... who come here expecting to get high wages, a feather bed and a bath tub."[1]

Since the railway companies and other labour-intensive industries needed labour for the rapidly expanding economy, the Canadian government adopted an immigration policy which allowed for a cheap and stable work force. It called for a labour pool in which low-status, unskilled and exploitable immigrants prevailed. In short, the new navvies would come from Eastern and Southern Europe.[2]

Immigrants from Russia, the eastern provinces of the Austro-Hungarian empire and southern Italy were deemed particularly desirable. They were seen as obedient and industrious, well-suited to the heavy work on the grade. Immigration officials especially encouraged the recruitment of Slavs. At that time not only were they considered racially superior to Mediterranean people, but these east Europeans were mainly peasants who accepted the work primarily as a way of acquiring land. Since many in government thought Canada had the greatest need for farmers to settle the western territories, these eastern Slavs represented ideal immigrants. They could work seasonally with the railways, save money and eventually attain their own land. On the other hand, railway employers, while they welcomed all labour, had a preference for southern Europeans, especially Italians. Since Italians did not generally homestead, but stayed more or less as unskilled labourers, the contractors and railway officials preferred them, especially those from the region south of Naples. As one CPR employment agent explained so adroitly: "If we have the Italians ... there is no danger of their jumping their jobs [at harvest time] and leaving us in the lurch."[3] In addition, employers thought that Italians did not integrate readily into Canadian society, which meant a greater insulation from trade unionists and other unwanted influences.

After 1905 when railway construction got fully underway, thousands of unskilled Slavic and Italian workers entered the country and when construction began on the Kettle Valley Railway in 1910, hundreds came to the Okanagan for work. Exact numbers are difficult to determine, but the local papers in Vernon, Kelowna, Summerland and Penticton repeatedly identified Italian crews, Russian navvies and Austrian labourers, Austrian being a catch-all term for the Slavs who came from the old Habsburg Empire.

THE ITALIANS, A CONTEMPORARY DESCRIPTION

The Italians ... comprise an important constituent among the workers in camps and on railway construction throughout Canada.... The Italian navvies must go about their work in their own style. While not fast, they are, nevertheless, very steady and consistent and accomplish much in the day's labour. While, usually, men of small frame, it is surprising what physical adaptiveness they display. They do not hesitate to undertake the heaviest manual work, and, although at times their physical tasks seem beyond them, yet grit and purpose seem never to desert these agile men. There is something in the companionship of the big gang that appeals to an Italian. He works best alongside his compatriots where he can still dwell within sound of his mother tongue. Invariably the camp-man from Italy is peaceful, very methodical, well-behaved and drinks little.

Nor are the Italians of the camps always homogeneous. A sharp cleavage shows too among this class of workers; there is the 'Naples' type or southern Italian and the northern Italian.

From Naples ships the man, short, swarthy, alert and keen.... The human traits are always near the surface among this class of Italian workers; noise and talk, general contentment varied with an occasional song and with laughter, usually marks their working hours; this, however, may be varied as suddenly with words of irritation followed as quickly, at times, with acts of revenge.

The northern Italian is different. Bigger physically, he is distinctive in appearance; also fairer in complexion, he is usually quieter-toned and invariably he is literate; he brings with him the instincts of his race, artistic, genial and versatile, but passionate too.

Edmund Bradwin, *The Bunkhouse Man*

These navvies were not the only ones who worked on the KVR. Many came from Scandinavia. The Okanagan papers and government reports frequently mention the Swedes, often in the same sentence as Italians and Austrians. The *Summerland Review,* for example, reported: "Almost all the men engaged on the work are of foreign birth, the majority being Scandinavians, Austrians and Italians. They speak English more or less brokenly." The *Vernon News,* for its part, commented that the "men, chiefly Swedes, Austrians and Italians" were

Navvies preparing to blast, possibly in Myra Canyon or near the Adra Tunnel. The box, labeled dynamite, contains fuses and sticks of explosives. A pick and other tools rest nearby. The rail cart loaded with rock will be pulled along the temporary tracks and tipped to one side, dumping the material into a low spot on the grade. The man smoking a corn cob pipe had paid ten cents for it in the contractor's commissary.

Northwest Museum of Arts & Culture, Spokane, Washington

some of the ones who had gone on strike in May 1913. Arthur Schacht, one of the subcontractors, testified before the BC Commission on Labour that his men were "at present mostly Swedes and Russians."[4]

Other nationalities also arrived. The *Grand Forks Gazette* wrote about some: "Special coaches with men for construction work on the Kettle Valley railway … have been passing through the city [Grand Forks].... P. T. McCallum, chief immigration officer for the district, reports that the men being brought in are largely Americans, Austrians and Germans and are a very good class."[5] A story which circulated later in Penticton told of several Greeks who, after working the American railroads, came to the Okanagan to work; someone advised them, however, to change their names to more English sounding ones so they could get better jobs. Apparently it worked. The ethnic diversity was impressive. Reporter F. G. Tily gave a good summary after visiting one of the KVR camps: "Here one sees quite a cosmopolitan crowd, Swedes, Austrians, Italians, Turks, Americans, English, Irish, Scotch [sic Scottish] and occasionally a Frenchmen and of course a few Chinamen."[6]

As for their recruitment, Canadian steamship companies took the lead,

This group of stiffs is working a rock cut, possibly above Naramata. The rail cart, located in front of and beneath the log platform, is loaded by the stiffs on top who drop the rocks into the cart. The horse then pulls the cart to the closest low spot on the grade. As necessary, other navvies set charges and blast the rock. *Penticton Museum*

contracting with labour-intensive industries like the railways to supply workers from Europe. By the turn of the twentieth century thousands of their agents and representatives travelled throughout the continent advertising North American prospects and the advantages of travelling with their particular company. Once he had recruited them, the agent directed the new immigrants to a specific ocean port. Trieste, Hamburg, Rotterdam and Liverpool served as the major ports for Canada. This method proved very successful for the steamship companies and generated considerable work for their representatives. An agent in Italy, for example, boasted that he had recruited 6,000 people in one year and could have sent more.

The recruits, mainly peasants and farm labourers, left their homes for many reasons. They came from areas where agriculture was limited and backward. They departed farms because of primitive technology, low yields or restricted land tenure. They emigrated because they had limited employment opportunities. They had heard, of course, about guarantees of plentiful work, stories of ready money and tales of marvellous opportunities. Not infrequently grand promises enticed them. For example, this idealistic description of working conditions in a Canadian railway camp once appeared (not for the KVR):

> *Life in the camps is strictly teetotal.... But the feeding provided is not only unstinted, but of the best obtainable and on a scale undreamed of by the navvy in this country.... There is an unlimited choice ... of fresh meat, fresh vegetables, groceries, butter, eggs, milk, bread and fruit.... After work, the men amuse themselves to good purpose, with sing-songs, fishing and shooting during the long summer.*[7]

Such promises surely appealed to the second and third sons of a poor peasant or just as likely to the peasant father himself.

Different representatives frequented the de-mobilization offices of the Russian army and recruited those mustering out. One scheme of interest to British

THE SLAVS, A CONTEMPORARY DESCRIPTION

As workers on construction they display definite characteristics: slow and immobile, lacking initiative; rather careless of personal appearance; with but limited mechanical ability; not quarrelsome except when liquor is about; easily brow-beaten, for the foot of despotism has cowed their spirit; just plodders in the day's work — withal, that pliant type that provides the human material for a camp boss to drive.

When seen to advantage the Slav as a camp-man is of medium stature, thick-set, with moustache usually, not graceful in motion and with something of a sullen expression on his broad face. There are other things that impress one when first meeting him in the mud cut on the grade; cowhide boots smeared with gumbo reaching to the knees, a peaked cap that bespeaks the barrack life not far removed, uncouth trousers and coat with old-land fastenings, unshaven face — with the dull resentment of the hard-heel showing from eyes, joyless-looking and suspicious. But, on further acquaintance, there is latent there the quiet strength, the unpretending courage, the perseverance and the staunchness which we like to think of as the very essence of our own Canadian character. By virtue of these good qualities and given fair conditions, the Slav can and does succeed even as a railway navvy.

Edmund Bradwin, *The Bunkhouse Man*

Columbia's southern interior concerned the Doukhobor leader, Peter Veregin, who announced that he planned to recruit 10,000 Russians for railway construction in the province. Although nothing came of this particular undertaking, Russian workers did come from Vladivostok to work between 1909 and 1913. The timing and circumstances fit perfectly for the KVR and it likely benefited from this flow of humanity.[8]

Any navvy who made his own way to the Okanagan found work since the railway faced a chronic shortage of labour. But what about those just arriving from offshore or those who did not have the resources to travel to the Okanagan? How did they manage to get to the site? Enter the private, unregulated employment agencies, conspicuous in most towns, especially those near labour intensive sites. For the KVR contractors, Calgary and Vancouver were of special importance.

A typical agency was plain looking and strategically located, often at a corner adjacent to a railway station or ocean port terminal. Its outside walls and windows had notices plastered about: "Men Wanted"; "Construction Labourer Required"; "Railway Contractor needs 100 men." Usually a chalk board gave further details while erased items implied or showed considerable activity. Occasionally the agency levied a charge for specific information or assessed a finder's fee paid by the prospective labourer, depending on the agency and the employer.

Once the recruit and the agency agreed upon the work, the new labourer generally signed a contract which stipulated his rate of pay and the price for room and board. Sometimes it included a clause or two about overtime and Sunday work for extra pay. A section common to most contracts encouraged the recruit to stay on the job for three to six months. If he did, any expenses associated with getting to camp would be refunded. This inducement was an attempt to offset the rapid turnover which usually saw as many men leaving the camp as arriving.

This clause about staying three or six months reflected a common problem for the men employed by the agency. The distance to the camp meant incurring substantial railway and steamboat fares. Making it even more difficult, the recruit typically had no money. So the company introduced its resolution: the employment agent, in agreement with the employer, advanced the fare, plus meals, accommodations and incidentals if needed. The entire amount would then be deducted from subsequent wages. Sometimes the agency even supplied tobacco and other inducements.[9]

Generally, the system worked well enough as verified by Arthur Schacht, a subcontractor near Naramata, when he spoke to the BC Commission on Labour in May 1913: "I went to the Coast about ten days or two weeks ago and brought in

SCHEDULE OF COMMISSARY PRICES

Blankets	$ 4.50 pr.
Grey sheets	2.50 pr.
Comforters	2.50 each
Gloves (canvas)	.15 pair
Gloves (leather)	1.25 to 1.75 pair
Handkerchiefs	.15 each
Jumpers	1.75 each
Tan shoe laces, 45"	.20 pair
Matches	.05 box
Mittens	.40 to 1.75 pair
Hungarian Nails 4 & 1/2s.	.20 package
Overalls	1.50 pair
Pipes, cob	.10 each
Shirts	1.50 to 2.50 each
Shoes - High Grade	6.50 and 7.00 pair
Half soles	.50 and .60 pair
Sox [socks], cotton	.15 pair, 2 for .25
Sox [socks], wool	.30 to .40 pair
Suspenders	.50 each
Tobacco, T&B and Myrtle Navy	.30 plug
T&B 5 pkgs to lb.	.25 pkge
Brier 9 pkgs to lb.	
Prince of Wales	
Bull Durham	.25 for 2
Old Chum	.25 pkge
Payroll	.15 straight
Towels	.35 each
Underwear	1.50 to 3.50

P. Welch, Railway Contractor, Vancouver

a bunch of 58 men [all Russians]. I had to advance their fares.… Anytime I need a large bunch I go to the employment office." He added that the employment agency had charged $1 per head, a fee paid by the men. Schacht further noted that in his experience the employment agencies had shown very good judgment in selecting the men.[10]

Not all employment agencies were alike, however. Some paid particular attention to the foreign-born worker, blessed as he was with strong arms and a broad back. Sometimes representatives of the agencies met arriving ships at the gangway. Others managed to board the vessel before docking. The newly-arrived, of course, expressed great delight at the news of prospective work. After a quick trip to the agency office where they signed up, the recently-recruited moved on to camp. Not surprisingly, these recruits arrived with little more knowledge of Canada than when they left Russia, Austria or Italy.

Another common practice occurred with the smooth-talking fellow countrymen, familiar with the language and experienced in the Canadian method of hiring. He recruited and took charge. The Italians had a particular bent toward this system, calling the practitioners, the *Padrone*. This countryman found the labour, either at home or already in Canada and supplied railway contractors like the KVR with reliable men. But the *Padrone* provided more to the contractor than just the important labour. He acted as the disciplinarian for the workers, often sending along a bilingual Italian foreman who controlled them through his knowledge of both languages. This relationship may have led to extortion and intimidation, but it also provided a crucial service for the new navvy. The *Padrone* helped facilitate his countryman's stay in Canada. He organized steamship tickets, sent earnings back to Italy, arranged for familiar food and above all, guaranteed work. Railway officials welcomed it and welcomed the Italian labour, as witnessed by the many who worked for the KVR contractors.

The unregulated employment agencies, not surprisingly, sometimes abused the system. The worst exploitation occurred on other sites, although the stiffs on the Kettle Valley Railway were not left unscathed. Since employment agencies received $1 to $2 for each man signed and delivered, the process required that these men actually turn up on the site. To assist their railway partner, the agency often hired someone, a scout or mancatcher, to escort a crew of men to the camp (as witnessed above with Schacht and his 58 men). There were stories, however, mainly in the east and on the prairies, where groups of men were put into sealed railway cars with armed guards to ensure they did not desert. That astute observer, Edmund Bradwin, who himself worked in the camps, wrote about cases of men handcuffed and manacled to the seats of their railway car.[11]

These stories were not exaggerations. The Nelson *Daily News* reported on this story from Moose Jaw:

This group of stiffs is working on a small cut with the aid of a rail cart. Once loaded, the horse will haul the "spoil" along the temporary track and dump it at the next low spot on the grade. *Penticton Museum*

A few days ago a train ... stopped at Boharm and just as it was gaining speed on its westward journey a sensational shooting affray took place. It appears that a large number of Russians were being taken to British Columbia to work on extra gangs and were locked in their cars, without having had anything to eat for two or three days. At Boharm they broke open two of the cars and tried to escape. An unknown person fired six shots and three of the men were hit, although none seriously and all got away.[12]

Another abuse and a common allegation from the navvy, involved the collusion between the agency and the foremen. The boss would discharge members of his gang and replace them with other men who had paid the agency for a job. The agency and the foreman then split the fee paid by the new recruits. This practice was not unknown on the KVR.[13] Moreover, a labourer might get a contract stipulating certain conditions only to discover when he got to camp that the foreman had different plans and different expectations. If the recruit tried to quit, he was sometimes held until he paid off his debt acquired in travelling to the camp. Or if he got back to the employment office and demanded his money back, the agency chased him out. No wonder the navvy called employment brokers "sharks."

If in doubt about how the men viewed these agencies and their supporters, one of the stiffs, writing in the BC media summarized:

> *Oh Canada! Canada! The sharks in town charge a dollar for these jobs; there are costs [to the site] ... and the stiff walks ... to camp. It's a great life, isn't it? And yet the people of this country allow ... these parasites who run employment bureaus in Vancouver and elsewhere to live in luxury and comfort while they themselves [the stiffs] have got to pay for the right to work. And they boast, the Canadian does, that he's a great race and Canada a great country. After hell, yes.[14]*

Even the government task force charged with examining labour conditions in British Columbia concurred. After touring the province, including the Okanagan, the Commission on Labour confirmed the abuses and recommended changes in its 1914 report:

> *The commission finds that the private employment agencies are unsatisfactory and is convinced that in many instances the managers of these agencies and the foremen of contractors share the commission fee of the employment agency, the result being that laborers are often discharged in order to make way for new men. It recommends that it be made a penal offence to engage in this practice.[15]*

The report further recommended publicly operated, no-fee labour bureaus.

Clearly the agencies committed wrongdoings, but the contractors also encountered problems with recruits who abused the employment system. The *British Columbia Federationist*, a trade union publication, even sketched out the issues:

> *It has long been the custom of the immigrants and others who desire to come west to sign contracts with the railway companies in order to get free fare. Just as soon as they arrive they break their contracts almost with impunity. According to railway officials in the city [Calgary] at present, the practice this season, so far, has been more prevalnt[sic] than in former years and as a result many gangs have been greatly depleted.[16]*

Unlike the stiff, however, the employer had a ready friend in the courts and an ally in the judges. Those who attempted to manipulate the KVR contractors received swift punishment for their transgressions. The *Kelowna Courier* carried this story in October 1912: "A quintette of Italians who were convicted of attempting to 'eat' the Kettle Valley Railway Co. out of fares to the camps and several days' board, were sentenced by Magistrate Boyce on Monday to 30 days in Kamloops gaol."[17] In May 1913 the *Penticton Herald* reported on several men accused of "Yumping their Yob," one of whom received a sentence of 10 days hard labour.[18] Later in September Kelowna's newspaper reported:

> *Four labourers of the Kettle Valley construction rank and file, were haled [hauled] to the Provincial Court on Monday by Constable Emmott on a charge laid by one of the contractors on the line, who claimed [they] had been advanced railway fare from Vancouver and then refused to work on the line. The men all pleaded guilty to the charge and were dismissed on the understanding that they will return and work out their indebtedness to the company.[19]*

Once the stiff arrived in camp, having survived his journey, the sharks and any other hardship, he discovered that his camp had divisions, not the ones which separated him from the bosses, but the ones which separated him from other workers. Camps had two distinct groups, the whites and the foreigners.

The term "white" implied two things on the KVR. On one hand it signified the white race. The KVR charter, for example, stipulated very clearly that "white labour shall be exclusively employed by said Railway Company, its contractors, agents, servants and assigns." This discrimination against Orientals unmistakably reflected the prevailing mood in British Columbia.[20] With some minor exceptions (a few Chinese worked as cook's helpers), the Kettle Valley Railway employed no Asian labour.

In the context of railway and KVR construction, however, the term "white" had an additional connotation. It designated the higher levels of manual labour and it was associated with particular ethnic groups, especially those who spoke English. Edmund Bradwin, who worked in numerous railway camps, wrote about these "whites." It always meant, he said, the Canadian-born, whether French or

THE STIFF, BY R. KLINK, A RAILWAY MAN

Have you ever toiled in camp with a bunch of railroad "stiffs"? Only those who have done it can know how hard their life is and how ill paid for their labor. They earn a stake of a hundred dollars, perhaps less, after three months' weary work away from civilization and they hike it to the city for a round of pleasure and debauchery. They are a rough, stolid class of workers, but they are straighter than some well-groomed, smooth-tongued men you meet in church on Sunday whose only reason for being there is because it's 'respectable.'

British Columbia Federationist, July 27, 1913.

Noon hour for the stiffs, somewhere between Myra Canyon and Naramata, possibly in 1913. The man second from the right casually holds several sticks of dynamite and some fuses while his one companion holds an axe and the other pours something from a bottle into a tin cup. The man second from the left holds a tin cup and has something on his fork. Five of the men are sitting on boxes, probably dynamite *boxes.*   *Penticton Museum*

English, as well as new arrivals from the British Isles and Americans from across the border. Usually it included the Swedes, which also meant Norwegians and sometimes Finns and it encompassed, as Bradwin concluded: "Any other foreign-born nationals who by their intelligence, their skill as workers or sheer native ability, have earned a recognition on their individual merits."[21]

On the Kettle Valley line Bradwin's definition found confirmation. One of the KVR workers gave his definition of "whites" when he testified before the BC Commission on Labour in 1913. After commenting on the importance of separate camps for white men and foreigners, a Commissioner asked: "What do you understand by a white man? A[nswer]. Canadians, Americans and Englishmen. Swedes and Germans are all right. Italians should not go under the name of white men. Neither should Japs, although Japs are cleaner than lots of white men. Still the white men don't care to be in the same camps."[22]

Foreigners, then, meant everyone not recognized as white. Bradwin stressed that the term, as applied to navvies, did not imply a slur on their nationality. It was primarily a generic term, used for those who did the mucking and heavier tasks on the rail line. Bradwin's list of foreigners included Ukrainians, Poles, Czechs, Slovaks, Bohemians, Austrians, Lithuanians, Ruthenians, Serbs, Croats, Bulgarians, Macedonians, Russians, Galicians, Hungarians, Italians and smaller numbers of Turks, Syrians, Armenians, Jews and some Germans (after 1914). He commented further that Orientals and Sikhs were also classified as foreigners but they were not allowed to build the railways any more.[23] Whether the point that the terms Bohunk, Polak, Douk or Hunky, as commonly used in the camps, was not a slur on nationality may be debatable, but the distinction between "whites" and foreigners certainly reflected the times. The distinction between the various groups also found reflection in camp life, which is our next consideration.

----

[1] Donald Avery, *"Dangerous Foreigners": European Immigrant Workers and Labour Radicalism in Canada, 1896 - 1931* (Toronto: McClelland & Stewart, 1979), 26.

[2] McCormack, 7.

[3] Avery, 27.

[4] "Railway Camps," *Summerland Review,* November 29, 1912, 1; "Laborers Strike on Kettle Valley Line," *Vernon News,* May 8, 1913, 1; "Labor Commission Meets at Penticton," *Vernon News,* May 15, 1913, 1.

[5] "Activity on the K. V. Line," *Grand Forks Gazette,* June 22, 1912, 1.

[6] F. G. Tily, "Massive Rock Cuts on Kettle Valley Railway," *Penticton Herald,* January 25, 1913, 1. The Chinese were probably camp cookees as Orientals were not allowed to work on the line. While First Nations people often laboured on other railways they do not appear to have worked on the KVR.

[7] Avery, 38.

[8] Ibid., 27.

[9] For further information on recruitment and contracts see Bradwin, 54-59.

[10] Testimony of Arthur Schacht, May 6, 1913, Penticton, BC Commission on Labour 1912-1914, BCA.

[11] Bradwin, 60.

[12] "Starving Russians Break from Cars," *Daily News* (Nelson), April 8, 1913, 1.

[13] Schacht Testimony, BC Commission on Labour. The Commissioner commented to Schacht: "We have been informed that these employment agents sometimes send out a bunch of men to different camps and have an arrangement whereby the men are discharged and others take their places and the employment agent gets half the fee?" Schacht responded: "I have heard of it, but not in my own experience."

[14] "Railway Camp Life Depicted By One of the Many Thousands," (letter by R. Klink, Vancouver), *The British Columbia Federationist,* July 27, 1913, 3.

[15] "Report of the Labor Commission," *Vernon News,* March 12, 1914, 5.

[16] "Railway Company Might Try Paying Decent Wages and Better Working Conditions," *The British Columbia Federationist,* May 23, 1913, 3.

[17] "Police Court," *Kelowna Courier,* October 30, 1912, Supplement.

[18] "Men who 'yumped yob' appear before Beak," *Penticton Herald,* May 17, 1913, 1.

[19] "Police Court," *Kelowna Courier,* September 4, 1913, 4.

[20] When J. J. Warren signed an agreement with the BC government on February 28, 1910, the contract stated: "That in the construction of the three lines of railway specified in the second paragraph B of said Agreement [including Midway to Penticton], white labour shall be exclusively employed by said Railway Company, its contractors, agents, servants and assigns, unless otherwise permitted by the Lieutenant-Governor in Council." BC Commission on the Pacific Great Eastern Railway, BCA.

[21] Bradwin, 92.

[22] Testimony of Hugh Standford McMulen, lather and shingler, May 6, 1913, Penticton, BC Commission on Labour 1912-1913. Although McMulen mentions "Japs," there were no Japanese working on the railway.

[23] Bradwin, 104 - 111.

CHAPTER V

THE CAMPS: NECESSARY AND BASIC

The navvy and other rail-workers may have spent 10 to 12 hours a day on the job, but the rest of their time they required a place to sleep, eat and prepare for the morrow. Since the grade where they laboured was usually some distance from a town, housing the various crews building the KVR required camps. The men needed sleeping quarters, kitchens, dining rooms, toilets, supporting outbuildings and the various paraphernalia to sustain a construction site. The resultant camps, however, were not permanent facilities, as evidenced in their construction. Generally they existed for a few months only, although the tunnel camp above Naramata operated for nearly a year and a half. Either the contractor or the railway provided and maintained the facilities, depending on who had responsibility for the occupants. As for quality, on this section of the KVR, including those in Myra Canyon, the camps were no better or worse than those found on other construction sites of the time.

According to officials of the BC government, five kinds of railway camps existed: one each for engineers, bridge-builders, tunnel and rock men, steam-shovel crews, and finally, grading gangs.[1] This general break-down possibly suited other parts of the province, but on the Hydraulic to Penticton section there were seemingly only two major types of camps, with a third possibility not mentioned by the government officials. First were the camps for the professionals, including the various engineers and their auxiliaries; second came the construction camps for navvies; and third were the scattered small facilities built by the station-men, the lowest level of the subcontractors. What is not clear, especially in Myra Canyon, was whether different camps existed for the professionals and the navvies or whether a particular camp had instead two sections, one side for management and the other part for labour.

The professionals' camps included the facilities for the resident engineer and his staff charged with overseeing several miles of the grade. On the Hydraulic to Penticton segment, for example, resident engineers dealt with five to eight mile sections; Myra Canyon's five miles (mile 8 to mile 13) belonged to one such professional. The camps and facilities for these men were quite good. Usually they consisted of cabins constructed of logs or lumber covered with tar paper. The buildings had a sound roof, they included windows, the walls (if lumber) contained some insulation and the structure boasted a wooden floor. Each of the several men who occupied the structure enjoyed his own bunk as well as some private space. Occasionally the men used the facility as an office in addition to a sleeping quarter. The camps also included a separate kitchen and eating area for food preparation and communal meals.

Edmund Bradwin, that fount of information on railway camps, gave this description of an engineer's accommodations:

> There is a spic-and-span air about it all, the buildings themselves are well put together, often hewn inside and out, the walls chinked regularly and neatly plastered. The whole surroundings have an air of consideration and thoughtfulness for the comfort of the dozen or more who dwell there.... [The men] have single bunks with plenty of good, clean, heavy blankets. The cleanly surroundings have their effect on the inmates, who invariably reflect these conditions by rigging up box spittoons, thus helping to keep the floor clean. Five to eight men ... will have a small bunkhouse to themselves - whereas, on the other hand, a building of similar size in the construction camp ... will do duty in housing thirty or forty inmates.... There will be plenty of windows, higher doors, good level floors and walls whitewashed or covered with white line-paper. These will be brightened, often, with pastings from some magazine or weekly paper. [2]

Bradwin's description rang true on the KVR. One resident at MacArthur's, a camp west of Penticton, called it one of the finest facilities he and his colleagues had ever seen and enjoyed. BC's health inspector also confirmed this general rule. He observed, several years in succession, that not only were the engineers' camps "quite clean," they had no need of an inspection.[3]

These camps also boasted excellent provisions. Bradwin again observed, "The supplies are ample and well assorted; the best of canned fruits, jams, pickles, oysters, prunes, apricots, peaches, dessicated potatoes, smoked meats and pork is supplied."[4] Some residency camps even developed a reputation for superb hospitality toward visitors, whether visiting engineers, officials of the line, contractors, churchmen, mailmen or anyone else who happened to arrive. Toward

The Crew at Residency No. 2 Kettle Valley Ry

This crew of professionals lived and worked at the Resident Engineer's camp, possibly in Myra Canyon about mile 13.5 from Hydraulic Summit. The work dress for professionals clearly differs from the clothing worn by the navvies. These men did not sleep in their clothes. The photograph also shows how the living and working quarters differed from those of the navvies. These cabins have windows with glass panes, the log walls are caulked to prevent drafts, the planked roof is covered with a heavy tar paper and the gables are also protected by tar paper.   *Northwest Museum of Arts & Culture, Spokane, Washington*

Naramata, one of the camps, in fact, established such a fine reputation that the good citizens from town frequented it for its excellent meals and comradery.

Quite different were the arrangements for the station-man, the small time subcontractor who had "contracted" with someone further up the hierarchy to work one or more stations of the grade; a station consisted of 100 feet of the right-of-way. Not infrequently a group of navvies, from two to ten, maybe more, negotiated a price to finish so many stations. With a piecework rate, the faster they worked the more money they accumulated. In their quest to save dollars, of course, the less they spent on accommodations, food and other essentials, the more money they amassed.

These men often made their own camps by the side of the grade. Sometimes they built a shack or two, more often they erected tents, usually ones rented from the higher level contractor. Four or five men slept to a tent. If there were several structures, they used one for cooking. Usually one of the group acted as cook, although not infrequently they took turns preparing very basic meals.

Food consisted of whatever they could acquire and prepare, plus the game they obtained from hunting (there was ample game on the KVR sections). Now and again, if they possessed enough money, the station-men ate with the stiffs. Some even lodged with them. After all, the station-man was not much different from the navvy, just a bit more daring and prepared to risk his labour and a contract price against the elements and the difficulties of the grade.

This type of labour was common on all Canadian railways and certainly existed on the KVR. The valley newspapers and local game wardens provided ample evidence of station-men activity, especially in connection with food. The KVR workers, for example, especially the Italians, were frequently mentioned as hunters, obviously shooting game for more than sport. Deputy Game Warden H. J. Blurton, for example, noted in June 1913: "Sullivan and I brought Leo Batrino, foreman of [an] Italian *station gang* [my emphasis] into Kelowna, also took in two witnesses who had seen four Italians belonging to this gang carrying a deer and had seen parts of a deer around this Italian camp." Batrino, incidentally, soon found himself in court, convicted of hunting offences and ordered to pay a hefty $100 fine or spend three months in jail.[5]

Bradwin has suggested the necessities for station men to commence work. For a group of eight men under normal circumstance he said they needed these items as their start-up supplies:

4 bags flour	1 granite pot
50 lbs bacon	1 box prunes
30 lbs coffee	1 box raisins
25 lbs sugar	24 plugs tobacco
25 lbs bread (immediate use)	1 half-barrel pork
2 cases condensed milk	1 half-barrel sauerkraut
50 lbs butter	3 bread pans
50 lbs beans	1 case tomatoes
1 stove (4-lid camp stove)	1 coffee pot
8 tin cups	8 tin plates
10 knives and forks	3 boxes matches
10 bars cheap soap	24 candles
4 wooden barrows	8 axe-heads and handles
8 shovels	2 boxes dynamite[6]

The individual arrangements for the station-men or the clean, fairly spacious camp for the engineers contrasted sharply with the facilities for the navvies. As with other aspects of railway construction, a correlation existed between ethnicity and the standard of treatment. Government inspectors in British Columbia repeatedly discovered that "foreigners" regularly lived in the most crowded and unsanitary accommodations.[7]

The camps for the stiffs, housing 50 to 200 souls, were clearly temporary and were subject to a constant turn-over of labour. They received only basic attention from the contractors. Although variations appeared from contractor to contractor, the *Summerland Review* provided a good, local description: "A typical railway camp has been laid out in Mr. H. Hodson's lot, east of town [Naramata].... In the side of the hill is a very fine cellar for storing supplies. Near this is a large stable for the horses and mules. Then there is a bunk house, eating house and cook house, not to mention a number of tents belonging to individual members of the party."[8] Although this account did not mention the toilets, the shed for black powder and explosives and the blacksmith or tool shop, it provided an accurate enough depiction.

In the Okanagan, as elsewhere, the bunkhouse, accommodating 30 to 60 men, served as the dominant camp feature. Its walls consisted of logs chinked with moss and clay. It measured roughly 25 by 60 feet with a roof fabricated from poles covered with heavy tarpaper or tarpaulins. This roof construction, unfortunately,

George Chew's camp 11, above trestle 8 (mile 86.55). The camp buildings reflect the winter conditions. The log walls are chinked to prevent drafts, all have heating stoves with chimneys and the roofs are solid, made of planks covered with tar paper. Two of the buildings have a clothesline between them full of laundry. The long building to the right is the bunkhouse, a prominent feature in each camp. Easily obtainable water flows in a creek at the foot of the hill in the foreground. The building in the distance possibly contained explosives. *Northwest Museum of Arts & Culture, Spokane, Washington*

offered limited protection from the rain and snow if the covering tore. Rough-sawn planks or poles laid on their sides made up the floor where dirt quickly collected. On some railway sites double bunks (i.e., two men to each bunk level) lined the sides and end of the building and sometimes the stiffs were obliged to pay for the hay which served as a mattress. The KVR camps, happily, provided bunks for each man, although some double ones did exist. A stove occupied the centre of the building while another section accommodated several barrels of water and a number of small basins and cheap soap which allowed the men to wash up before each meal.

The most striking thing about the bunkhouse was the absence of light. The dwelling had only two small windows in the gables, making the entire interior dark and dungeon-like. It also meant the men engaged in a brisk trade in candles, especially in the shorter months of the year. Although the darkness made it difficult to read or write or even see, a small redeeming advantage, as the men pointed out, was that it was warm. Windows made a bunkhouse cold.

There were also other noticeable features. After extended use it invariably became infested with vermin. Nits and lice got into the bedding while other creatures of the dark crawled around the floors day and night. Another prominent characteristic was the smell. The poor ventilation became evident in the evenings when the stiffs hung out overalls, underwear and other clothing to dry. Imagine

The bunkhouse was a prominent feature in each construction camp. Measuring roughly 25 x 60 feet it was home for 30 to 60 men. Bunks lined the inside walls with a limited common area in the middle. Since there were no windows, except two small ones in the gables at each end, visibility was limited. A stove provided heat while the rafters served as a place to hang wet, soggy, sweat ridden clothing to dry. Limited ventilation meant pungent odors while too little cleaning allowed nits and lice to flourish. *Penticton Museum*

A CONTRACTOR PRAISES HIS CAMP

Gilbert Brandt, railway contractor

Q. Have you good camps?

A. I have good camps. I'm very sorry I didn't meet you down there so I could take you around the camps. Lots of space in them. In Camp 2, the dining room is 70 feet long and twenty feet wide, of logs. The kitchen is 20 x 24, all of logs. I have two sleeping rooms 64 x 22 and then I have two tents 18 x 24, put up with boards to 8 feet. The biggest number that has been in that camp is something like 120 men. That was only about two weeks. There's been an average of something like ninety-five to a hundred men. Camp 1 is practically the same way.

Q. How do you arrange the bunks? Two tiers?

A. Two tiers on one side and one on the other

Q. Do the men sleep two in a bunk?

A. No. All single bunks. Some men come in and like to sleep together. The board is fixed so it can be taken out and make a double bunk of it. Would be about 4 ½ feet wide. They come sometimes in parties and like to sleep together because they have more bedding. Simply take that board out and have a double bunk.

BC Commission on Labour, May 6, 1913, Penticton

50 men, bodies unwashed, each with sweat laden garments and mucky boots, sleeping on old straw, covered with musty, lice ridden blankets. As one veteran of the grade remarked: "I can assure you that the stench that protrudes from those places between 11 o'clock at night and 4 a.m. is enough to knock a man down."[9] The provincial health inspector put it a bit more delicately, but no less meaningfully: "The question of the ventilation of bunk-houses is a somewhat difficult one.... Clothes are frequently dried in the same room as that in which the men sleep and unless the windows and doors are kept open, which is impossible in bad weather, the atmosphere becomes very close."[10]

The issue of sanitation assumed a prominent place in the railway camps. Only months before the KVR construction, primitive and unsafe facilities generally marked all sites. One health inspector, after visiting a railway camp in the north, reported on the lack of toilets: "The sanitary arrangements are nil ... [and] as a result the ground was filthy."[11] This shortcoming resulted in contaminated water supplies followed by typhoid fever epidemics, a reality not uncommon to the camps. Fortunately, the KVR sites had improved toilet facilities or at least, well placed ones and a more carefully monitored water supply than many railway camps. This improvement meant not a single reported case of typhoid fever on the Hydraulic to Penticton section.

The navvy might tolerate primitive living conditions but he required good, solid food, not as a benefit, but as a necessity. He could not meet the heavy work

A UNIONIST PERSPECTIVE ON THE CAMPS

John J. O'Connor, IWW organizer

Q. *Mr. Mackelvie. How are conditions in regard to the sleeping accommodations and so on?*

A. *I am glad you asked me that. I intended getting to that. Take table board. The impression is that Mr. Schacht has very poor table board. I don't know whether it is on account of the Chinamen he employs or the poor board. Most of the other camps the board is not good but we have done worse on the coast. The sleeping accommodations are something fierce in some of the camps. The bunks are arranged one over the other, for two men that probably never seen each other. The men just take any place that's left and furnish their own blankets. 90 cents a day for board and dollar a month for hospital....*

The BC health regulations and that law is posted in some of the bunk houses, requires them to have bath house and sanitary conveniences, a certain amount of air space and other arrangements. In very few instances is it lived up to. Some camps are better than others. Some pretty bad and some not so bad. I was in George Chew's camp last winter.... I was then working on the grade. They heard the inspector was coming so the word was sent around to clean up. They threw away all the old clothes and some of the men's clothes that they had to go out in the snow afterwards and get them. About noon the inspector came around and went into one camp and looked at the ceiling and said 'Fine. You're making a proper job out of this.' The next bunkhouse he made the same remark. Then he turned around and went away.... He had dinner at the camp and left.

BC Commission on Labour, May 6, 1913, Penticton.

load without an ample intake of calories. Employers, therefore, including those on this section of the KVR, fed their men well. In some cases they even went further, competing with one another to attract and keep the men. As Bradwin wrote: "Camp-men will go where chuck is best."[12] In the case of the Kettle Valley, the contractors paid close attention to the navvy: "Last Wednesday morning, in Gilbert Brandt's camp 3, the boss called all out. None went out and the boss went in to find out what the trouble was. The men told him they wanted a new cook – and it didn't take him long to concede [to] the demand."[13]

Picture, then, a camp of 100 men, each engaged in heavy manual labour for ten hours a day and each needing a daily intake of 5,000 to 6,000 calories to maintain his activity. That gives some idea of the magnitude of this business. This regime meant not just the cooks working full time to prepare breakfast, lunch and dinner, but it included a constant stream of freighters and haulers bringing in supplies: salted pork, smoked meats, bacon, beans, flour, vegetables, dried fruits, cheese, coffee, canned goods of every description, raisins, prunes and fresh fruits in season. The camp bosses clearly had to pay close attention to logistics.

A cook house crew posing in front of the dining tent, probably near Naramata about 1912. The man on the left, "playing" the broom as his guitar, is George Gribbler while the navvy on the far right is Aug Larson. The Pioneer tent, manufactured in Vancouver, was a common sight in the KVR construction camps.   *Penticton Museum*

Other considerations, about which we do not think today, required attention. Those in charge of food had no refrigeration so any fresh fruits or vegetables had to be eaten rather quickly. Or if they planned fresh meat dishes, they had to butcher the animals on site, cook them and preferably consume everything to avoid leftovers. Until the meat was actually cooked, however, it needed protection from flies so kitchens were supplied with boxes or shelves covered with fine wire netting for protection.

Then came the bread. One of the amazing features of the navvy diet was the amount of bread consumed, vastly exceeding today's standard. Most of the men, especially the Italians, could and did eat a loaf a day. The loaves were not small either, often two feet long and eight inches thick. Providing this staple for several score men required enormous amounts of flour and supplies, not to mention a significant time commitment. It also meant a constant use of the bake ovens. Bradwin explained how they worked: "The oven is first fired red-hot, the coals are

A CONTRACTOR'S VIEW ON CAMP FOOD

Arthur Schacht, railway contractor near Naramata

Q. What do you charge for board?   *A. $6.00 a week.*

Q. Do you get even at that?   *A. No. Hardly.*

Q. You couldn't possibly do it for any less?   *A. No, I could not.*

Q. Do you consider this board is good enough?

A. Well, it's very good board. When I am away I'm always getting back to camp to get a square meal. Very good board. The best that can be got.

Mr. Harper: Do the men complain about it?

A. Sometimes. That's one of the general complaints in camp. When they leave and you ask them what's the trouble, the board's on the bum.

Q. Plenty of fresh meat?   *A. Yes. Always.*

Q. Vegetables?

A. Yes. Fresh beef, ham, bacon, smoked meats, sausage, vegetables, lots of the hardy winter vegetables and when spring vegetables come we get those.

Q. What do they complain about?

A. I don't know. There's general complaint. Nobody knows what about or why.

BC Commission on Labour, May 6, 1913, Penticton

then hastily scraped out and a large portion of dough is placed on the heated clay bottom.... The loaves thus baked are ... well-crusted and most toothsome."[14]

One of the interesting features to be found today along the KVR stretch west of Myra are the stone ovens. Nearly 30 have been discovered, sometimes one to a camp, although not infrequently two or more per site. These ovens, probably built by the Italians who were known for their mortarless stone work, remain as testimonials to the extensive food preparations required for the navvies.

How did contemporaries and inhabitants rate the temporary camps? A reporter for the *Summerland Review,* for example, heaped praises on them:

> *The camps are fitted up with every thought for the comfort and cleanliness of the workingman and the meals which are served up, make the ones which are served in some of the hotels and restaurants seem very expensive at fifteen or twenty cents. There is everything in the food line that any man could wish for and fresh meat is brought up twice a week. Anything else that the men require, such as tobacco, snuff or clothing, can be bought at the commissary, at town prices.[15]*

An organizer for the IWW, on the other hand, expressed scorn. He emphasized the need to improve camp conditions and the food. In an interview with the *Penticton Herald,* he was told that a government inspector had recently visited one of the KVR camps on the east side of the lake and had reported favourably on the sanitary conditions. The IWW man retorted with a "Ha"! There were no wash houses, he asserted. Then he explained why the men demanded that the contractors supply blankets. Much of the disease, he contended, came into camp by men forced to pack their blankets from place to place, thus carrying germs in with them and contaminating the bunkhouse.[16] Which account gave the true picture? The contractor Schacht offered his ambiguous response when asked how the stiffs found his camp: "Lots of men say its one of the best camps they were ever in. Others say its one of the rottenest. You can draw your own conclusions."[17]

The camps, especially the contractor's headquarters, bustled with activity. Aside from the KVR officials, the bosses, the navvies and the cooking crews who frequented the sites, a myriad of other folks joined them each day: freighters, blacksmiths, police, game wardens, fire wardens, health inspectors, religious and secular missionaries and the gawking visitors who came from who knows where. A brief comment on each adds further particulars on the camps and the life there.

Crucial to the camps were the freighters and haulers. In addition to the food they carried, they brought baled hay and oats for the stable; dynamite and black

The candy wagon   Ed Lind   Teamster

Two examples of freighters and haulers for the construction camps. The "Candy Wagon" with teamster Ed Lind is a low-bed wagon pulled by two mules. Since it cost a penny a pound to haul goods to the camps, the luggage in the wagon probably belonged to professionals and maybe the "whites" who had more possessions. The blanketstiffs generally carried their goods on their backs. The second wagon is pulled by a four horse team driven by teamster Norman Mitchell. His colleague, C. H. Bacher, stands on the hill beside him. Mitchell is possibly moving the camp as he is sitting upon a pile of canvas and his wagon is piled high with goods, including a saw horse protruding from the side. The man with the rifle is probably a hunter, not someone protecting the goods by riding "shotgun"! *Penticton Museum*

powder for the blasters; mackinaws, boots, rubbers, socks, shirts, shoepacks, stationery, painkillers, mosquito-oil, snuff and tobacco for the store; and for those who could afford it, their baggage. The shouts of the teamsters reverberated across the camp early and late.[18]

Since humans and horses or mules did most of the work, the metal tools and implements they used required maintenance and care. Therefore, the blacksmith was crucial. Most camps, especially the headquarters sites, had a shop with anvils, sledges, big link chains, steel rods for drills, parts for the dump carts and spares of every kind. The draft animals, of course, required shoes, which meant not just a blacksmith but also a farrier. After a blast, the shattered, sharp rocks could injure an animal so the horses' and mules' hooves needed good protection and regular maintenance.

At George Chew's Headquarters near Myra Canyon, the BC Provincial Police maintained a station. Constable Fred Emmott made regular trips up and down the line from Hydraulic to Penticton. According to his son, when Emmott joined as a lawman patrolling on the KVR, he received a badge, a revolver, a pair of handcuffs and 65 dollars a month, a good wage in those days. His son later wrote:

The farrier at one of Grant Smith's camps, possibly the camp of G. Hunt, blacksmith. The mule has its harness on so it is ready to go to work as soon as the farrier finishes clinching the nails of the shoe.   *Penticton Museum*

Some of the horses used by the crews working for George Chew in Myra Canyon. Since they were not hobbled, was there an unseen fence to contain them?

Northwest Museum of Arts & Culture, Spokane

Constable Emmott made his patrols on horseback, riding along the grade or on the tote-road that paralleled the right-of-way. His clothes were the usual garb of the day: a mackinaw jacket, whipcord trousers and a Stetson hat styled half-way between the stiff-brimmed military type and a cowboy's 10 gallon. His revolver was always tucked decorously out of sight and his 30 - 30 rifle usually remained in the Kelowna police barracks.... His most-used piece of equipment was his black notebook, in which he recorded the 'particulars' for his reports.[19]

Members of the Kelowna branch of the Provincial Police also made regular trips to the Myra camps while constables from Naramata frequented the sites up to Chute Lake. They sought out the liquor peddlers, evidence of any prostitution and instances of petty crime. They also conducted investigations into the all-too-frequent deaths of those on the job.

Two stories give an indication of police activity as well as the local attitude toward the foreigners:

The other case before the beak [magistrate] was that of Dominick Davidio, a son of Italy who was conveyed down from the railway camps by Constable Emmott, who discovered that Dominick was carrying around on his person a lethal weapon, to wit, one five shot 32. cal Smith & Wesson revolver.

Dominick was fined $10 and costs and the gun was confiscated. In addition to the fine, a lecture on the evils of carrying dangerous weapons was given Davidio by the magistrate, who pointed out that the sentence might easily be a much heavier one; in fact, deportation from the country was an ordinary result of such a conviction. Davidio absorbed the words of wisdom in an unenthusiastic manner, but promised to be a real good Neapolitan in future.[20]

The second case, reported in January 1914, observed:

In the provincial Police Court yesterday, two Russians from Chew's Camp, KVR, were up before the Magistrate for fighting. Constable Emmott arrested the men after the mix-up and brought them to town. When ranged before the beak, one of the men, with a typical Russian and therefore unwriteable name, pled guilty to stabbing his compatriot in the leg with a knife, the act being one of self defence, he claimed. He was fined $25 and costs or a total of $37.75. The wounded party, a big wild-looking Cossack, with a reputation for being a 'buttinsky' [meddler], was fined $10 for assaulting the knifer and ordered to pay his own doctor's bill. He was quite peeved at the decision and maintained that he was a peace-loving individual, but the Russian interpreter wagged his head and solemnly advised the subject of the Czar to 'come through.' And Khabarovskovitch, etc., cussed like a 'drosky' driver [a freighter], but dug up the coin.[21]

Visiting the camps on a regular basis, game wardens came to check on gun licenses and hunting permits. They frequently spent the night and occasionally acted as backup for the policeman on duty. In August 1913, for example, one game warden reported:

On patrol on horseback all day amongst the construction camps, returning to Chews Headquarters camp. This evening Emmott had a telephone call about an Italian cutting scrape [fight], the Italian who had done the cutting had struck out of the hills, Emmott caught him and left him for me to look after all night, while he went into the hills to the camp where the row had taken place.[22]

The wardens also had to deal with local citizenry concerned that the stiffs hunted out of season, either killing too many animals or scaring off the game for others. At one point the Kelowna Board of Trade discussed the issue at considerable length, agreeing on the need for more wardens for the KVR. One of its members expressed the view that "every tenth man up in the camps had a

Hunting was one form of sport for the professional crews working the KVR, as is seen with this man, his gun and his bobcat trophy. Many of the station-men and navvies, however, hunted for food to supplement their diet.

Northwest Museum of Arts & Culture, Spokane, Washington

gun." He did not know what they were doing "if they were not killing the game, much to the detriment of local residents."[23]

The fear of fire brought others to the camps and the grade. Fire wardens patrolled the line daily. Their great worry and the anxiety for the contractors, obviously came from the blasting, the sparks from machines and locomotives and the activity of the construction crews. All these activities, of course, occurred in a region of dry grass, heavy timber and flammable bush, a clear formula for fire. But those who observed the grade had another cause for concern. As the Forestry Branch reported, the greatest danger arose from the building of tote roads when long lines of slash remained lying about. Since this flammable material was close to the camps, where fires often burned unattended, the hazard was great.[24]

Beginning in the spring of 1913 the BC government and the KVR agreed jointly to pay for fire patrols. They arranged that each day, including Sundays, between the hours of 7 am and 6 pm, wardens made at least one round trip along the line, "instructed to pay particular attention to public traffic ... and to campers and construction employees passing to and fro." During the height of the fire season

AN UNUSUAL STRAW-BOSS.

Human derelicts, once sturdy craft in the navigation of the stormy cruise of life, frequently face Magistrate Guernsey and other administrators of the law and in Wednesday morning's police court, arraigned for being D & I [drunk & intoxicated], appeared John Reggan, former hero of the Afghan war, a Victoria Cross man, formerly sergeant of the Dublin Fusiliers, at the time of the war in question, known as the Bombay Fusiliers. Sergeant Reggan has been employed in the Grant Smith construction camp at Naramata for some weeks. While there he was in charge of a gang of Austrians.

He was badly scarred above the eye when he appeared before the court on Wednesday, but he assured the magistrate that he was a man that could take care of himself and that he had left several Austrians looking much worse than himself. Reggan, V. C., is getting along in years. He has passed the three score mark and the straight soldierly back is beginning to bend with the weight of years. But when in a reminiscent mood, the old fire of the born fighter still kindles in the old blue eyes, as he recalls the stirring tales of the famous 'Lord Bobs' victorious march, 600 miles from Cabul to Candahar, which he participated in and for which he wears on his breast the Afghan medal, coveted trophy of a bloody campaign.

Over a glass of liquor, which has been the stumbling block in the old fighter's life, John Reggan, told the Herald *of his six years of service, most of which was under that peerless leader of men, "Bobs," the idol of Tommy Atkins and rightly called the most popular man in the British army. Near the blood-stained mud walls of Cabul one night Reggan saved the lives of two scouts from his own regiment, who returning from a reconnaissance, had fallen into the hands of a party of Afghans. For this the highest honor to which a soldier can aspire, was awarded Reggan and for serious wounds which he received in the encounter, he was given a pension.*

Penticton Herald, November 1, 1913

they doubled the patrols. As a result, during the entire construction era no fires of consequence occurred.[25]

Health inspectors also made occasional visits to the camps, although these visits did not occur on a regular basis. Generally the inspectors found all in order or they directed the contractor to make minor changes. One may wonder, however, how much attention they really gave to health issues when considering the Chief Sanitation Inspector's annual reports. For several years after 1912 the text of each report did not vary; word for word they were identical.

Other visitors included Christian preachers holding Sunday services, representatives of the Woman's Christian Temperance Union handing out pamphlets and leaflets, delegates from the Railroad YMCA providing literature, nuns from the Sisters of Mercy collecting for a foundlings' home, organizers for the Industrial Workers of the World recruiting for the "one big union" and the townsfolk who came regularly for the good food.

The camps clearly embraced a multitude of activities. The multilingual chatter among the men, the clatter and banging of tools, the clang of the hammer on the anvil, the neighing of the horses accompanied by the shouting of the teamsters, the squealing of pigs as they awaited slaughter, the bosses barking out their orders for the day and even the ringing of a telephone mixed with the aroma of baking bread, the stink of the toilet and the waft of foul air emanating from the bunkhouse. These represented the sights, sounds and smells of the camp and they served as the backdrop for the men as they marched off to moil for the cause.

---

[1] Second Report of the Provincial Sanitary Inspector, BC, *Sessional Papers,* 1913.

[2] Bradwin, 87.

[3] Sanitary Inspector, *Sessional Papers*, 1913, 1914 and 1915.

[4] Bradwin, 86.

[5] Daily Deputy Game Wardens Report of Deputy Game Warden H. J. Blurton, Station Mara, Okanagan district for Month of June 1913, BCA.

[6] Bradwin, 117.

[7] Sanitary Inspector, *Sessional Papers*, 1913, 1914 and 1915.

[8] "Naramata," *Summerland Review,* September 13, 1912, 2.

[9] McCormack, 4.

[10] First Report of the Provincial Sanitary Inspector, BC, *Sessional Papers,* 1912, BCA. See also Bradwin, 75-85, for other particulars on the bunkhouses.

[11] McCormack, 4.

[12] Bradwin, 179.

[13] W. M. Kress, "Camp Workers Rebel," *Industrial Worker*, April 24, 1913, 1.

[14] Bradwin, 131.

[15] F. G. T. [Tily], "K.V. Ry. Grading At Trout Creek," *Penticton Herald,* October 5, 1912, 8.

[16] "IWW Organizer Fined For Trespassing," *Penticton Herald,* March 15, 1913, 1.

[17] Testimony of Arthur Schacht, May 6, 1913, Penticton, BC Commission on Labour, BCA.

[18] Freighters charged a penny a pound to carry supplies to the camps.

[19] N. W. Emmott, "Policing the Rails," *Canada West* (1979), 16.

[20] "Police Court," *Kelowna Courier,* October 23, 1913.

[21] "Local and Personal News," *Kelowna Courier,* January 22, 1914, 5.

[22] Daily Report of Deputy Game Warden H. J. Blurton, August 1913.

[23] "Board of Trade Monthly Meeting," *Orchard City Record*, June 26, 1913, 1.

[24] "Precaution Against Fires," *Grand Forks Gazette,* July 12, 1913, 2.

[25] Correspondence between Clyde Leavitt, Chief Fire Inspector, Board of Railway Commissioners, Canada, Ottawa; H. R. McMillan, Chief Forester, Ministry of Forests, Victoria; and J. J. Warren, April & May, 1913, BCA.

CHAPTER VI

THE WORK:
ITS REWARDS AND ITS RISKS

Railway construction was not easy. Hours were long. Tools were simple. The rocks sharp and heavy. Flies and mosquitoes were constant pests. The Okanagan climate featured oppressive heat in the summer and fierce cold in the winter. Mishaps were frequent and accidental deaths all too common. If you were "white," then decent pay and some respect helped compensate for the hardships. If you were a "foreigner," however, it was the fact of having a job, not the wages, that compensated for the privations. The exploited, minimally paid, low- status navvy differed significantly from his white counterpart.

What sort of work did each of the groups do? The whites had tasks and positions which brought status of some kind. They had responsibilities as surveyors or crew members, walking-bosses, accountants, inspectors, camp foremen, store keepers or clerks who managed the supplies and operational logistics. They included the cooks and their helpers (except for the occasional Chinese), the teamsters who hauled the materials and the bosses on the line. The whites also did most of the rock work, where skill in handling and setting explosives was essential for both safety and effective blasting. They operated the few steam engines and the occasional power drills used in boring the tunnels. Other whites worked on the bridges and wooden trestles where some knowledge of English was fundamental in directing hazardous tasks. Once the work of levelling the grade was complete, the whites manned the machines which set the ties and laid the steel and they crewed the ballast trains which stabilized the track. In short, the skilled work went to the whites.

The foreigner, on the other hand, did the heavy manual labour, the mucking and the toting. They did the "joe jobs" which required muscle, sweat and very few skills. They worked with pick, shovel, wheelbarrow and their hands. They grunted as they scraped to level the grade, strained as they picked up the rock, hurried to fill in the holes, struggled to dig the trestle foundations and pounded

Navvies working in a rock cut, possibly near Myra Canyon, 1913. After loading the rail cart with the "spoil," horses hauled the material to a nearby low place on the grade.The pry bars at the left are used to loosen rocks and soil. *Penticton Museum*

away on the spikes as they secured the rails. The work was tough, but without them the KVR and Canada's railways would not have been built.

Days were long and gruelling; work was distasteful and dangerous. Stiffs generally toiled a minimum of 10 hours a day, beginning at 7 am and they laboured six days a week. Sundays were set aside for rest as specified by legislation, although occasionally some work occurred, that is, until the Attorney General in Victoria took Warren to task for allowing it. His rebuke led to an exchange of correspondence where both parties accepted that KVR contractors could only engage in critical equipment repairs and essential maintenance on that day. But even then the rest day was not always observed, especially in the case of station-men who worked to a contract, not as wage earners.

While muscle power definitely built the railway, the navvy had some help. His hand tools generally came from the Gandy Tool Company of Chicago and were of good quality. He used the ubiquitous shovel, pick and rake. Help also came from horses and mules hooked up to small rail cars which moved along narrow, temporary tracks hauling rock from the high places to fill the holes at the low spots. These cars, also ubiquitous, frequented the many blasting sites or wherever one found a rock cut under way. Further, the stiffs used the hand drills, a chisel-like metal rod, employed to drive the tunnels. The work of boring required a three-man crew, one stiff to hold the drill while the other two took turns hammering it against the rock. Between each strike of the hammer the first man rotated the drill a quarter turn. On a good day they bored through five feet of rock.[1]

Three men normally made up a drilling crew. The man with the gloves in the middle held the drill while the other two alternate in striking it with their eight pound sledge hammers. Between strikes the man in the middle turned the drill one-quarter turn.   *Penticton Museum*

Aside from muscle power, another great facilitator helped build the KVR – black powder and its associates, nitroglycerine and dynamite. The contractors used an enormous amount of explosives, especially since the rock between Hydraulic and Penticton proved extensive and hard. As many as five boxcars of explosives might go into a single blast, after which the navvies scurried about with pick, shovel, scraper and cart to clear and move the rock.[2]

The *Penticton Herald* explained in rather thespian terms how this part of the construction worked:

> *One is confronted with towering heights of solid rock, which have withstood the ravages of countless ages, but it cannot stand in the path of the railroad. A big burly Swede is noticed drilling into the rock, preparing for blasting. You will hear him shout 'fire,' and see the men all scattering to a place of safety. Presently there is a terrific explosion and a mighty upheaval and great masses of rock are scattered in all directions, thereby moving, in a few seconds, that mighty solid structure which has stood through all time. What an enormous power that dynamite has, but the men handle it quite unconcernedly. Now the laborers will handle this loose rock into cars and it is taken away to fill in the low places.*[3]

SKILLED AND UNSKILLED LABOUR, AS SEEN BY GILBERT BRANDT, RAILWAY CONTRACTOR

Mr. Jardine: Do the strikers get anything extra, the men who strike the steel?

A. We generally pay them a quarter extra, because we call them skilled labor. In our class of labor maybe twenty men are shipped from Vancouver and in that crowd maybe five or six are better than the whole fifteen. For instance, I have some Italians come from Calgary. Took them down in the rock cuts and I believe the biggest part of them never had held a shovel before. Some of them got down on their knees when shovelling. That shows the kind of labor we get sometimes. Its pretty hard to pay wages to that class of labor.

Mr. Stoney: It doesn't take very long for them to learn how to handle a shovel?

A. It takes quite a while before they're able to do any good for you.

Mr. Jardine. What's the weight of those hammers they strike with?

A. Eight pounds.

Q. A man can keep that up ten hours?

A. Yes. To a man that gets used to handling a hammer it's only play work. Get a green man at it and he works a hardship on himself.

BC Commission on Labour, May 6, 1913, Penticton

Although the men may have handled the explosives "quite unconcernedly," numerous accidents and occasional deaths resulted from misuse or failed settings. The valley newspapers contained many stories about the dangers of blasting: "Another serious accident occurred in Hildebrant's camp, Monday afternoon, when two men who were loading a hole for a shot, were more or less seriously injured about the face and eyes. Explosion was no doubt caused by tamping the powder." Kelowna's newspaper carried a similar but more tragic story: "A dreadful accident occurred at the Railway works near Naramata yesterday afternoon in which three Italians were killed and six others badly injured. The cause of the disaster was the premature explosion of four boxes of dynamite." Or again: "By the premature explosion of 20 sticks of dynamite in a cut near Kimble's Camp …

a labourer named P. A. Granroth Anderson was immediately killed and another man injured. Anderson was literally blown to pieces by the terrific explosion."[4]

Sometimes the blasting fatalities had a more bizarre cause: "Louis Johnson, a Swede ... was blown to pieces while thawing out a stick of dynamite.... It appeared from the evidence that Johnson took the dynamite and placed it in a tin of water. This he put on a fire, which was burning nearby, for the purpose of thawing out before using it for blasting with. He had hardly done so when a terrific explosion occurred and Johnson was literally blown to pieces."[5] Meanwhile, another story explained the dangers of smoking on the job: "A Swede, named Anderson met death in a shocking manner while employed at one of Grant-Smith & Co's camps last week. He was seated on a keg of dynamite when the contents suddenly exploded and blew him out of all recognition.... The explosion is thought to be due to the victim's smoking."[6] The most bizarre fatality, however, was reported in the *Penticton Herald:* "One of the most extraordinary and determined cases of suicide occurred on Wednesday morning last, at about 6 o'clock, at No. 1 camp of the KVR construction party, when John Olson, a sub-contractor, it is alleged, laid down, placed two sticks of dynamite upon his chest, ignited the fuse and calmly waited for the awful explosion which ended his earthly career."[7] Self-imposed or not, working with explosives on the KVR and other railways entailed considerable danger.

The crews not only engaged in blasting, tunnelling and levelling the grade, they had to erect the trestles. As explained earlier, the trestles of Myra Canyon were framed first in Carmi or Naramata, then transported to the end of the rail line for assembly. The contractors used two methods of construction, quite similar to the two methods used in re-building the several trestles that burned in the 2003 fire. One technique, used mainly on the smaller trestles, employed a railway crane which dropped each bent, i.e., the structural framework which supported the trestle transversely, into place. Once crews had secured each bent with horizontal stringers the crane moved further out and dropped the next one into place, until all bents were positioned and secured. The second method, used for longer trestles over deeper ravines like the east and west forks of Canyon Creek, employed sky-lines. In this case crews strung cables across the chasm and secured them. Running lines then lifted and set the wooden beams, girders and timber into place. Steam powered "donkey" engines operated the drum winches on the running lines.

Whichever method of trestle construction was used, it held inherent dangers. Valley newspapers again carried accounts of accidents and fatalities:

The two men are preparing a "coyote" or hole for blasting, probably for the east tunnel in Myra Canyon (mile 85.7). They will fill the opening with blasting powder. After the explosion the navvies will remove the rock which will be used as fill along the grade.

*Northwest Museum of Arts & Culture,
Spokane, Washington*

This photo taken in Myra Canyon at the moment of the blast, either near trestle 11 (mile 85.9) or trestle 18 (mile 84.9), carries the caption: "Jenson & Co.'s coyote shot."

Penticton Museum

(*Above*) The two men are standing atop the rock which has recently been dislodged as the result of a coyote shot. The rocks, some of a very good size, must now be removed by the navvies in order for the grade to progress.

Northwest Museum of Arts & Culture,
Spokane, Washington

The two men are tipping a very large rock off a rail cart, near Naramata. The man on the left has a bar which he uses to operate a jack while the second man struggles to stabilize the cart. A service road goes around the side of the hill on the right.

Penticton Museum

(Left) A crane on a partially built trestle lowers a bent for the other story. This was one method of construction along with the sky-line procedure. The crane lowered the vertical supports, the bents, into position and the workers secured them with horizontal stringers and diagonal bracing timbers. Then the trestle platform was built so the crane could move further out and position the next bent. This trestle has three stories.

Penticton Museum

(Below) Trestle 6, Myra Canyon (mile 87.9). The construction of this trestle began in June 1914 and was completed in just over a month. A work train brought the building materials from Carmi to the edge of the gorge. The cable or sky-line across the chasm then carried the assembled timbers which were lowered into position. The first story of the trestle is visible in the valley floor on the right. Several men on the platform to the left, are discussing the progress.

Penticton Museum

Still another life was added to the toll which it seems must inevitably be exacted in the building of a railway, especially such a one as the Kettle Valley, which abounds in difficult and dangerous work. A man named Henry Mathieson, a Swede, was precititated [sic precipitated] last Sunday morning from the top of a trestle bridge which spans the Canyon and his mangled remains were picked up fifty feet below. [8]

Death, when it came on the line, rarely arrived without pain and gruesome detail.

Eventually the contractors finished their portion of the work. The tunnels and rock cuts were completed, the trestles built and the grade readied. Now came the job of laying the steel. For this the KVR employed its own crew, usually about 100 men, whites and foreigners, bosses and navvies. They worked from a train pushing the tracklaying machine (called the pioneer) and pulling the rail cars packed with ties and rails. A journalist described how it worked, employing again the theatrical language of the time:

In the middle is a locomotive. Along each side ... runs a wooden trough, suspended in air, bottomed with rollers. From the cars, into the trough at the right of the train, men are throwing ties; into the trough at the left, rails. A steady current of ties and rails flows forward over the rollers of the troughs, forward all the way to the Machine. The Machine stands like a gallows frame at the front of the foremost car. Ahead of it crosswise on the grade, the ties fall ... whereupon, with long wooden arms extending forward from its bony frame, with steel cables for tendons and compressed air clutches for hands, the Machine lifts the rails, swings them and lays them down on the ties. [9]

The navvies then quickly sprang forward and pounded in the huge spikes which held the rails in place. They had to move fast since the train inched onto the rail a fraction of a second after it was fully secured. Later the ballasting train and its crew filled the space between the ties with gravel to stabilize the track. With the steel down and the ballast in place, another segment of the line awaited regular service.

The navvy who worked as a day-labourer on the KVR earned $2.75 per day, about the norm for railway work in that era. From his earnings he had to pay $6 per week for room and board and he had to pay down any debts incurred in travelling to camp or for his purchases in the company store. Itinerants frequently started their jobs heavily indebted to the company for transportation costs. Sometimes weeks passed before they actually earned money, so the stiffs frequently complained about working only for "grub and tobacco." Normally the

The tracklaying machinery described by young navvy Art Stiffe, quoted in Robert Turner, *Steam on the Kettle Valley*: "There is a gang on the end, keeps putting ties on the conveyor. Another gang are putting rails on this conveyor belt back behind. This boom is bringing the rail up here, forward…. They bring the rail out, the guys get on each end and lower it on the ties. Of course, prior to that time, the gang ahead has it all lined up…. They laid the ties down not too tight…. A guy comes along with a wooden gauge to space the ties. As soon as the rails are put down, two or three guys, they drive the odd spike but they don't drive many spikes at all; a couple of spikes here, a couple of spikes there. Just enough to hold it and that's all. 'Toot! Toot!' and she [the locomotive] pulls ahead a predetermined amount…. Then the next ties are going ahead and the next rail comes out."

Penticton Museum

(Opposite) These three photographs, taken near the Little Tunnel above Naramata, illustrate the process of ballasting using "Hart Convertible" ballast cars. The work car contained a steam winch and cable assembly. The cable ran over the ballast cars to a plow. The winch drew the cable and plow forward, causing the plow to force the ballast out the sides of the cars. The sides of the Hart cars were equipped with hinges and locking pins so that the cars could be loaded like gondolas with a steam shovel, but unloaded quickly and without a large amount of labour. (Description courtesy Barrie Sanford)

Barrie Sanford Archives and Penticton Museum

contractors paid them once a month, but if a man quit work between pay periods, as countless did, he immediately got his pay cheque, minus any debts and went on his way.[10]

Most neutral observers agreed that $2.75 a day was not the best wage, but the day-labourers often boasted a better time of it than their work-mates who laboured as station-men. These navvies, the final link in the chain of letting contracts, frequently had little to show for long periods of back-breaking work. As mentioned earlier, stations were 100 foot sections of right-of-way. Groups of itinerants, frequently foreigners, working as petty entrepreneurs, contracted to grade several stations and prepare them for steel. The undertaking usually required no heavy equipment, only muscle and simple tools like shovels, picks and wheelbarrows. Under favourable conditions they could make more money than day labour. As a result, some enterprising stiffs thought they had an opportunity and they were encouraged by the higher level bosses to work long and hard at their own small projects. This system clearly benefited the contractor. As one of them observed: "Ten station men will take out more rock in a month than twenty men, yes, sometimes more than thirty men, working for wages." But the charges and fees that plagued day labourers also applied to station-men and seriously depleted any profit. They still had to sort out travel costs and expenses, accommodation and food, tools and incidentals. One stiff complained that the chances of becoming rich on station work "are just as good as prospecting for gold in a pile of sawdust."[11]

Although the rail labourer was male, neither very young nor very old and was, according to Baldwin, "splendidly endowed with rugged strength and native hardihood," the hazards of the job made medical services essential. The men wore no protective gear, no safety harnesses, no helmets, no steel-toed boots and often no gloves. All this simplicity of dress made the stiff susceptible to serious injury from the smallest accident. Further, although any heavy construction project will produce accidents, rock work on the rail-beds of British Columbia caused remarkable carnage. The KVR was no exception.

The stiffs paid $1 per month toward medical care, the services of which had been tendered out. On many lines the chief contractor arranged for medical treatment on his section. In the case of the Kettle Valley, however, the company itself took the stiff's monthly dollar and engaged the services of a Vancouver practioner, Dr. Kerr, who had responsibility for the entire line. In the Okanagan and environs Kerr set up railway hospitals and clinics in Carmi, the Mission (then separate from Kelowna), Naramata and Merritt. For his section, Grant Smith

COMPARISON OF WAGES IN THE OKANAGAN VALLEY

Kelowna:

    Canning Company:

Skilled white labour	$ 3-3.50	/day;
Unskilled	2.50	
Chinese	1.80	
Women	1.50	

    Stationery Engineer: 100 /month

    Cigar Factory:

Cigar makers	25-33	/week;
Women	7- 15	/week

    City labour: 3 /day

    Farm labour: 3 /day (with board)

    Sawmill labour: 2.50-3.50 /day

    Oriental: 2.25-2.50 /day

Penticton:

    Common labour: 3 /day

    Farm labour: Chinese: 2 /day

    Orchard men: 3 /day

    Cultivation & irrigation: 4 /day

    Lathers & Shinglers: 3.75 /day

    Municipal Employees:

City clerk:	150	/month
Asst city clerk:	75	/month
City engineer:	150	/month
Asst city engineer:	75	/month
Police:	90 - 125	/month

    Railway construction:

Cook	85	/month
Cookee	35-50	/month
Skilled labour	3.75-4	/day
Unskilled	2.75-3	/day

The BC Commission on Labour, 1914.

located the main medical facility on today's Collett Road in Okanagan Mission. Here, a doctor and two nurses worked from a clinic behind the old Bellevue Hotel and dealt with cases which arose in the camps from Hydraulic to Chute Lake plus referrals from Naramata. The hospital had an important asset in that it was not far from the wharf, the transportation hub, where men and supplies unloaded and moved to the higher level worksites.[12]

The secondary hospital in Naramata serviced the camps east from Penticton to Chute Lake. It too was manned by one doctor, usually a young intern or recent graduate and one male nurse and was housed in a cottage opposite Mr. Mulford's butcher shop. Medical cases went there first, but if quite serious, the doctor transferred patients by steamer to Okanagan Mission which had better facilities. Occasionally cases went to Penticton's four-bed hospital run by Miss Hancock. The Naramata clinic was originally led by Dr. Whitehouse until May 1913, when he was succeeded by Dr. Will L. Robinson, son of Naramata's founder. Assisted by his nurse, Toni Manzini, Robinson remained there until the hospital closed in March 1914.[13]

How good was the medical service for the stiff on the grade? It certainly did not prevent accidents or deaths on the line, but the doctors did visit the camps, inspect

NOT MUCH PAY FOR A MONTH'S WORK
John J. O'Connor, IWW organizer

Mr. Jardine. What would be a fair estimate of the amount necessary for you men to live by the week? How much can a man save out of $2.75 a day?

A. If they are working for $2.75 a day and charged 90 cents for board, taking into consideration that they can't work every day on account of weather conditions, $30 or $35 is as much as they can make and from that they must buy the necessary clothes. They are compelled to buy them in camp not because its compulsory but quite a ways from town.

Q. Do you mean to say the total powers [earnings] of the average man are $35 a month?

A. That's my experience of the best a man can do working on the grade.

Mr. Mackelvie. That's his savings power?

A. $35 is as much as I made in any month.

BC Commission on Labour, May 6, 1913, Penticton

sanitation facilities, insist upon some changes and generally oversee the men's well-being. Warren claimed in May 1913: "So far as the hospital arrangements are concerned they could not be improved, proof being in the fact that although over 3,000 were employed all winter, no epidemic of any kind broke out."[14] On the other hand K. M. Kress from Spokane's *Industrial Worker* gave the contrary view:

Grant Smith's hospitals are the limit. A station man in Gilbert Brandt's camp 3 had his foot crushed with a rock. They took him to the Mission.... Inflammation set in.... During the night the fire went out, as they can't even afford to hire a bull cook and in the morning the man's foot was frozen, making it necessary to amputate his leg above the knee. In this hospital the patients have to pack in their own fire wood and drinking water; also they get very little to eat, in fact some of the men who come out are so weak from hunger that it takes them from two to three weeks to get back their strength.[15]

Not surprisingly, the employer and the employee presented dissimilar views. Perhaps contractor Schacht's earlier observation about his camp – it was either the best or the worst – could fit the hospital as well. It depended upon who made the observation.

In all likelihood the medical facilities reflected the times, just as the work undertaken by the stiffs mirrored the era. The exploited labour, the limited rewards and the high risks were not unique to the KVR, but were found on every rail line in North America. The particular rigours and hardships faced by the Kettle Valley toilers merely confirmed those other stories. Yet, like the others, they added immense value to the landscape, in this instance the Okanagan landscape. They were the stiffs who "built" this railway and enhanced the growth of southern British Columbia.

There is also another side to the story of their labour. These stiffs engaged in tasks markedly different from the standards today, tasks that many would now avoid. Not many today would undertake such arduous labour with so little gear for such nominal pay. Nor would many today entertain such a heavy risk of injury or the real possibility of a fatal accident. Not many today would live the life of the camp-man, sharing not only the impediments on his labour but the limitations of his leisure. His free moments away from the grade, as we shall see next, were not always calming or restful. In many respects his exploitation just continued in another form.

[1] W. J. Bowser, Attorney General, to Warren, August 8, 1912, Victoria, PMA.

[2] Sanford, 168.

[3] "Massive Rock Cuts on Kettle Valley Railway," *Penticton Herald,* January 25, 1913, 1.

[4] "Naramata," *Vernon News,* January 16, 1913, 6; "Three Killed and Six Injured," *Orchard City Record,* June 12, 1913, 1; "Fatal Explosion on Kettle Valley Line," *Kelowna Courier,* July 31, 1913, 1.

[5] "Attempt to Thaw Out Dynamite Stick," *Penticton Herald,* December 12, 1912, 22.

[6] "Town and Country Notes," *Orchard City Record*, July 31, 1913, 4.

[7] "A Deliberate Case of Suicide," *Penticton Herald,* March 9, 1912, 8.

[8] "Fell Fifty Feet to Death in Canyon," *Orchard City Record,* July 9, 1914, 1.

[9] McCormack, 8.

[10] For further reading on pay see Bradwin, 63-74.

[11] McCormack, 3.

[12] F. W. Andrew, "Early Medical Service in the Okanagan Valley," *The 12th Report of the Okanagan Historical Society* (1948), 128; Primrose Upton, "The History of the Okanagan Mission," *The 30th Report of the Okanagan Historical Society* (1966), 197.

[13] Andrew, 128, 132; "Naramata," *Vernon News,* June 12, 1913, 6; "Naramata," *Vernon News,* April 2, 1914, 8.

[14] "Movement Is Revolutionary," *Daily News*, May 9, 1913, 1.

[15] W. M. Kress, "Camp Workers Rebel," *Industrial Worker,* April 24, 1913, 1.

CHAPTER VII

OFF-DUTY:
WHAT TO DO AND WHO CARED

When not working, the stiff spent his time in a number of ways. He had clothes to wash and mend, boots to repair, hair to cut, letters home to write (or have written for him) and maybe some sleep to recoup. These activities represented the standard, even routine, things which required attention after hours or on Sundays. But there were also the other possibilities, always available, if only surreptitiously: gambling and drinking alcohol. As for a card game – the stiff had no problem finding one since there was a permanent game going on at each site. As for alcohol – if he was careful not to get caught, he had plenty of opportunity to buy and consume liquor. For those stiffs who left the camp and went on a spree, the nearby bars in Kelowna and Penticton beckoned, augmented by the ladies of the night, both pub and lady happily relieving the navvy of his money. Some bosses also indulged in these same activities but they also had access to respectable dances, special holiday celebrations, polite female company and sporting events.

Most camps welcomed any number of special visitors. Those like the social reformers, the citizen educators and the secular missionaries sojourned among the navvies and their bosses providing sustenance for the soul, relief from the tedium and hope for the future. They showed that it was not just the barmen, prostitutes and gamblers who cared about the stiff and his wellbeing.

The first group to pay attention and show interest in the navvy, however, were the purveyors of alcohol. The sale of liquor on the grade, not unexpectedly, was strictly prohibited. The bosses had a great fear that excessive consumption would cause unruly and violent conduct or as one Kelowna policeman put it: "[With alcohol] the mixture of nationalities inevitably engenders rows and fights." So the contractors banned it and the authorities vigorously enforced its prohibition. Yet wherever one found camps and isolated workers, one found liquor. Again, the KVR was no exception.

Alcohol came into the Kettle Valley camps in any number of ways, generally through outside bootleggers or by the men themselves packing it in. According to police reports, the authorities maintained a particularly watchful eye in the Canyon Creek area looking for liquor peddlers. They did not always locate the hawkers, but they did find the evidence. As reported by the *Kelowna Courier*:

> *On Wednesday news came in from Morrissey's Camp, No. 2 [in Myra Canyon], that an Italian had been frozen to death while returning to the camp from Kelowna. It seems that the man ... about 22 years of age, walked in the 14 miles or so, on Tuesday, to send away some money orders for his friends and also, evidently to bring up some firewater from town. He reached a spot about two miles from camp on his return trip and apparently lay down against a log to rest, as he was carrying a dozen bottles of whisky.... It was evident that he had simply gone to sleep, under the influence of the liquor he had absorbed.[1]*

Here lay an obvious lesson about the dangers of sampling one's own wares.

Another story had a much happier ending for the peddlers. On this occasion two Italians walking back to Morrissey's Myra camp encountered Constable Vachon of the BC Provincial Police. When the good constable asked what they carried, he discovered 16 gallons of whiskey and a good quantity of beer, a load which he immediately confiscated. After transporting men and spirits to Kelowna, Vachon delivered the two stiffs to the police court, but the judge released them when the prosecution failed to prove the men planned to retail the liquor. The Italians also countered their accusers by arguing a "plausible" case. They said the men in the

---

ALCOHOL

Arthur Schacht, railway contractor near Naramata

Q. Mr. Jardine: When your work is near these places that are licensed for the sale of intoxicating liquor, do you have any greater difficulty with the men?

A. Yes.

Q. Do you think if the number of hours were restricted or if the sale of liquor was shut off altogether it would be an advantage to the men?

A. Yes, I do.

Q. Mr. Harper: Do not a great many take liquor to the camp?

A. We have considerable trouble that way.

BC Commission on Labour, May 6, 1913, Penticton

camp had just "chipped in" on the expenses. Why, asked the magistrate? They planned a "grand celebration on Easter Day," came the quick reply. [2]

The local press outlined another variation for acquiring alcohol, although it pointed to the success of the law this time:

> Constable Graham brought off a coup that should slacken the energies of the liquor peddlers. A man with a pack on his back came from Naramata and was followed some miles back into the country where he cached his burden of liquor at a spot evidently agreed upon before hand. Later on a horse and rig driven by a young man ... came along and took up the hidden bottles with the intention of conveying them to the camps for consumption there. Constable Graham intervened, however, and made seizure of the liquor. [3]

The police triumphed and a public hurrah followed, but did it signal tough luck for the peddler? Perhaps it did for this bootlegger, but if true to form another soon stepped forward to fill the demand.

There was another side to the consumption of alcohol as well. When the stiff left the camp, either because he had finished his job, was fed up with the work or had been idled by the boss, he frequently spent a great deal of time and money in local bars. The drinking spree served as one way to forget the miseries of the job or the gloom in his life. As one valley newspaper noted when writing of a group "lounging around Penticton": They remained because they "are far too thirsty and desire to be near a slaking place."[4]

Brothels also played a part in camp life, although in the case of the KVR the prostitutes seemingly did not solicit close to the camps as was the case on other railway construction sites. The closest house of ill-fame for the Myra men took them to Dixie Auston. She had an establishment in the Mission, possibly on Benvoulin Road, a location certainly within striking distance of the camps. The stiffs further down the line could venture into a red light district which was a bit closer, as confirmed by the *Industrial Worker* from Spokane. In reporting on the trial of an IWW colleague, the *IW* cynically observed: "Thorne's trial depleted the treasury so the city fathers made up the amount by raiding the red light district, two miles from Penticton. Twenty-five stiffs were made to pay [a] $10 fine each."[5]

Another pleasurable, if somewhat illicit form of entertainment, came from gambling. The navvies played in the camps and they played on the spree. They played whenever and wherever an opportunity arose. Ted Logie, a young resident of Summerland who frequented the camps out of Naramata, often watched. Later he wrote:

They used to play after payday until one or two of the players had cornered most of the cash in camp, then they would drift up to the next camp and eventually the winners there would possibly end up in Kelowna where a bigger game was in progress twenty-four hours a day. They might stay lucky for awhile, but eventually the run of the cards would send them back to the muck stick or drill and they would start all over again. Seemingly that was the life they enjoyed. [6]

The *Orchard City Record* added its own story about stiffs and poker. This tale involved the Kelowna police chief and his night constable, both attempting to deal abruptly with systemic gambling. Singling out the Bunk House over the barber shop on Main Street, the pair of law enforcers sneaked up the stairs, grabbed the sentinel and scared him into silence. Then the two peace officers burst into the room, startling and scattering the players. They found a table covered with cards and piles of money and arrested seven Italians, all railway labourers, plus some others of "the class which preys upon them." The paper gleefully announced that after being "marched to the coop and brought up before the magistrate" the resulting fines for illegal gambling meant "enriching the city coffers by $164.50."[7]

While the navvies found their escapes in liquor, sex and cards, some of the bosses engaged in more genteel forms of entertainment – dances, holiday meals and organized sports. The valley's social columns frequently recounted stories of wonderful dances hosted by the railway people or the contractors. One such occasion involved joint sponsors, the KVR engineers and the staff of Grant Smith & Company. Not surprisingly, that evening's dance programme included such wonders as The Dynamite Drag, The Canyon Creek Crawl, The Tunnel Tango, The Work Train Wiggle and The Kettle Valley Kickup. The column concluded, not quite so creatively as the dance list, that "the affair was a most enjoyable one."[8]

WARREN, RELIGION AND SWEARING

J. J. Warren was apparently a deeply religious man. Once when he, in the company of his chief engineer, visited one of the camps, he overheard one of the navvies, engaged in a card game, use the Lord's name in vain because of his poor hand or poor play. Warren immediately went over and thoroughly rebuked the man for his cuss.

Story related to Barrie Sanford by an eyewitness

On another occasion one of the camp contractors threw an American style Thanksgiving Dinner for his staff and several local "gentlemen and ladies." In reading the newspaper account a picture of some comfort emerged, an image which contrasted sharply with that of the navvy:

> *The mess house was gaily decorated with flags that well suggested an international entente cordiale - the Stars and Stripes on the walls and the table decorated with the Canadian flag and the Union Jack. The menu was carried out by cooks who might well qualify as chefs and included such delicacies as Saddle Rock Oyster Soup, Local Barnyard Turkey, Queen Olives, Ham Cured Halibut a la Crème, Oyster Stuffey Cranberryee and a wonderful collection of rich cakes decorated with the Canadian flags in miniature. It may perhaps be mentioned that 'Mumm's Dry' figured not inconspicuously on the wine list.* [9]

The alcohol prohibition naturally did not apply to the bosses on their special

This picture, taken in one of the camps above Naramata, shows Ted Logie of Summerland (middle) with his KVR friends George Harmont on the right, Lou Bacher on the left and Bill, the timekeeper, swigging from the bottle. Although the picture is posed, it illustrates the illicit activity carried on by the navvies in camp. A few did carry pistols, many drank bootlegged liquor and many more played in the card games which were always in progress.   *Penticton Museum*

occasions while the menu attested to the fine cuisine frequently mentioned in connection with several of the railway kitchens.

For the professional staff with excess energy they had another outlet in organized sports. For two seasons in 1913/1914 and 1914/1915 the bosses fielded a basketball team in the Penticton league. For a time, they occupied first place. It was quite a different style of basketball from today, however, as seen in a recap of one match:

> *The game aroused more interest than practically any match played during the season.... The K V R took the lead from the start, running up thirteen goals through accurate shooting by Burgess and an excellent combination work by McKenzie. The bankers [the opponents] seemed to be unable to locate their goal until the last few moments in the first when McCoy, Glenn and Murray scored in succession.... The financial magnates came back strong in the second spasm and by brilliant shooting by McCoy and Murray and clever passing by Glenn and DeBeck, scored goal after goal. The KVR only*

Gilbert Brandt & Company's Camp 2 dining room. This picture, taken in January 1913, shows a set up for a special occasion (note the temporary benches and the tables decorated with paper flowers). Several of the kitchens in the camps above Naramata welcomed visitors and had a reputation for good food.

Penticton Museum

succeeded in securing three throughout the entire second half and the game ended [21 to 16]. [10]

The exercise, obviously not the scoring, provided the excitement.

The barman, the liquor merchant, the prostitute, the gambler and the policeman all showed an interest in the navvy for pecuniary and legal reasons, but others had a more tender concern for his welfare. Several religious and philanthropic organizations showed an active interest in him. For example, across Canada the Salvation Army cared for the itinerants, especially when down and out or when they had to recover from a spree. The Roman Catholic clergy looked after its French and Italian flocks while the Anglicans, the Methodists and the Presbyterians sent their missionaries into the camps and the organized reading rooms.

The most unique group, the Reading Camp Association (RCA), later known as Frontier College, undertook the most crucial and noteworthy work. Although not a religious organization, the association exuded the same Christian idealism that carried young men and women into the urban ghettos to help the immigrant poor. The RCA worked through volunteers, generally university undergraduates who laboured beside the men during the day and schooled them at night. They taught everything from basic English to university mathematics, although the bulk of their lessons were quite elementary. They sought not just to educate, but to Canadianize. The central, eastern and southern Europeans knew little of Canada and needed to learn about "our standards, our norms and our civilization," especially if they planned to remain in this country. This edification could

McCULLOCH AND SHAKESPEARE

McCulloch carried small editions of Shakespeare's work with him when he travelled. He had no need, though, to consult his books in order to recite famous lines. Stories abound of McCulloch visiting the work camps and joining the men around a fire in the evening. He would recite extensive passages from his favourite playwright and keep the men enthralled.

One might wonder, however, how much the Slav, the Austrian or the Russian understood. With his limited English, how much of Shakespeare did he grasp? It was probably McCulloch's manner and presentation that kept him enraptured; the words themselves made little difference.

Further evidence of McCulloch's love of Shakespeare comes in the station names he assigned in the Coquihalla region: Juliet, Romeo, Iago, Portia, Jessica, Lear and Othello.

happen by studying English, by gaining knowledge of geography and certainly by learning about citizenship. As part of their effort these labourer-teachers also established reading tents where navvies could leaf through newspapers and magazines, further familiarizing themselves with Anglo-Canadian literature as well as alleviating the boredom of camp life.[11] Although the RCA had no direct presence on the KVR, its spirit and philosophy clearly permeated the efforts of local churches, socially minded groups and philanthropic individuals.

The churches of Summerland took the lead in ministering to the navvies as early as August 1912. They gathered and distributed papers and magazines, sent their ministers to hold meetings, put on several music concerts and planned 50 book libraries for each of the nearby camps. They discovered that the literature was enthusiastically received, especially the magazines like *Canada* and *Sketch* which had lots of pictures. As the local paper reminded its readers: "There are a number of men who can speak English tolerably well yet cannot read our language and it is to those men that these pictures appeal."[12] At year's end in 1912 the committee responsible for this philanthropy rightly concluded: "The work is worthy of the support, material and moral, of every good citizen, irrespective of religious proclivities.... To the members of the various churches of Summerland an opportunity ... is presented of demonstrating that our professions of 'true religion and undefiled' is something more than 'mouthfuls of spoken wind.'"[13]

Shadows.

A group of surveyors at leisure, reflecting while being reflected.   *Penticton Museum*

While this work initially concentrated on the camps closest to Summerland, that is, north and west of Penticton, the committee planned to expand its endeavours to the east side of Okanagan Lake. Whether it ever did remains unclear, but others came to Penticton and travelled north and east towards Myra to care for the men. One of the important organizations which worked in these camps was the Railroad Young Men's Christian Association (RRYMCA). This organization, which had laboured among railway men in the US since the 1860's, had over 230 branches when its representative first arrived in the Okanagan in 1913. The RRYMCA was a common feature in communities that had railway yards or terminals. It provided beds, meals and showers in an atmosphere free of alcohol and other temptations. The RRYMCA also addressed the educational and spiritual needs of the navvies by offering courses, establishing libraries and organizing reading rooms. That explained why Mr. S. A. Smallwood of the Portland, Oregon branch, arrived in Penticton in August 1913. With the full support of both the KVR and the contractors, both of whom recognized "the value of his work for the moral uplift of the men," he spent some days visiting all the camps through to Hydraulic Summit. He also spearheaded a campaign whereby Penticton's churches and other organizations collected and distributed newspapers and periodicals to the men.[14]

About the same time in the camps closer to and including Myra Canyon, the

A visitor has arrived in his buggy at this KVR construction camp, near the Adra Tunnel (mile 113.9) and is greeted by a handful of inhabitants. This camp, built around a central square, contains the usual tents with clearly visible flies and log structures. The timber is unchinked. One bunkhouse with a chimney and three roof vents for air circulation is behind the tent on the right while a second bunkhouse, also with air vents, is located directly behind the first one. The ubiquitous wood pile in just behind the small dog in the middle of the square. *Penticton Museum*

Sunday activities often included a shave and a haircut plus other personal chores like laundry or writing letters home. Since many of the navvies were illiterate, the man who served as "letter writer" was a valued friend.

Penticton Museum

Woman's Christian Temperance Union (WCTU) of Kelowna began its work. Founded originally in the United States in 1874 to push for the prohibition of alcohol, it had quickly spread to Canada and established branches across the country, including several in the Okanagan. In the years since its founding the WCTU had also expanded its interests to include the education of the less fortunate. The two interests, prohibition and literacy, now guided the Kelowna branch as it undertook what it termed its "missionary work." Unlike the Frontier College, it did not restrict its literature to English. Its women acquired magazines and temperance literature in both Swedish and Italian which it sent to the Kettle Valley camps above Kelowna. Its members acquired copies of the Bible in Greek, handing them out to the men "who seemed glad to get them." Its adherents made calls on the bunkhouses in Kelowna which the railway men frequented and distributed literature amongst them. It persuaded local Christian ministers to hold religious services in the camps. It further solicited funds in order to buy foreign literature for the many stiffs who read no English. At its annual general meeting in May 1914 the executive trumpeted its accomplishment. Not only had they gathered large quantities of literature and sent them to the railway camps, those blessings had been accompanied by "20 comfort bags through the kindness of Mr. Henning."[15]

Other missionaries joined the scurry to the construction camps, but this time they came as Marxists and syndicalists, not as Christians. The now legendary Wobblies, the Industrial Workers of the World, arrived to organize and agitate for better working conditions. Since its founding in 1905 in Chicago the Wobblies had advocated long term social and economic reform and short term improvements. The IWW worked on the premise that capitalism was evil and could be destroyed by organizing the down-trodden workers into large industrial unions which welcomed all labourers. But more germane to those who toiled now, it sought immediate improvements in wages and working conditions. Its paper, the *Industrial Worker* promised: "The IWW will take the blankets off your back, Mr. Blanketstiff. It will make the boss furnish the blankets. And further, not only the blankets but springs and mattresses; yes and as we grow stronger, sheets and pillows. Just imagine yourself snoozing away, tucked up between nice clean sheets, with your head resting on a pillow and a good mattress and springs under you."[16]

Since its halls extended real help with food, shelter, news of work and occasionally medical attention and it accepted everyone, including the newly arrived unskilled immigrant, the IWW offered genuine hope at a time when not many others did. The Wobblies gained a good following in Western Canada, especially in the camps of BC But they also provoked great animosity among the railway companies and the contractors. Joined by the provincial government as a third detractor, company, contractor and bureaucrat vigorously and successfully defied the Wobblies, which was best exemplified in British Columbia when they overcame the extended 1912 strike on the Canadian Northern.[17]

In the Okanagan the IWW and its organizers arrived with the first KVR labourers in the summer of 1912, but they did not become very active until just after the new year in 1913. Not surprisingly, they brought their big message and their more immediate promises: "Every worker in British Columbia [should] rise up in rebellion against capitalist tyranny and by building One Big Union of construction workers force the thieving and murderous railroad contractors to cease their brutal attacks upon the workers." More immediately, the organizers in the Okanagan pledged to fight for higher wages, better food and improved conditions.[18]

Welcomed in the camps by the men, the Wobblies, not unexpectedly, were attacked by the contractors and the authorities, both physically and figuratively. The earliest incident near Naramata came in February 1913. As reported by the *Penticton Herald:*

After securing the men's consent to talk, they [the two Wobblies] were set
upon by the contractor and his family in an attempt to do them bodily
injury and drive them from the camp. Some of the men interfered and the
clubbing stopped, but the police arrived and placed Thorne and Mulder [the
Wobblies] under arrest.... A charge of disturbance on the public highway has
been placed against them. [19]

Thorne received a sentence of 30 days in jail and Mulder was released. A third associate, although not arrested, was run out of town by the police. A few days later another organizer in a nearby camp suffered a similar arrest for trespassing. He too was convicted and fined.

The IWW organizers, accustomed to such a reception, were not fazed and continued their work. They established Branch #335 in Naramata with the same Conrad Mulder (recently assaulted) as secretary and they built a union hall, located provocatively next door to the offices of head contractor Grant Smith. The Wobblies particularly focused their attention on the section just north of Naramata where the line doubled back on itself. This configuration meant that a number of camps were concentrated in a fairly small area making the work of organizing an easier task. But the IWW did not neglect those further up the line as they visited all the camps between Penticton and Hydraulic. Nor did they overlook the camps around Summerland on the west side of the lake. Within a short time rumours of a strike circulated widely. [20]

Work disruptions followed. At first they were small, although somewhat

During the construction era, Naramata served the KVR in several capacities: as a site for supplies to the contractors, an office for Grant Smith & Company, a union hall for the Wobblies and a drinking locale for the navvies. *Penticton Museum*

effective and clearly noticed. In the second week of March 1913 some 100 men left their camps on the east side of the lake, a move viewed in the press as preliminary to a general strike rumoured for the next week. "Practically the whole of the construction is now held up on the Naramata side," reported the *Greenwood Ledge*. Two weeks later most of the men at Gilbert Brandt's camp, also near Naramata, "struck work ... the ostensible reason being for an increase in wages." The *Penticton Herald* continued: "Steps have been taken by the Provincial and local police to prevent any disturbance of the peace and strict watch is being kept on strangers coming into town." Within another two weeks "owing to the discharge of an IWW man about 100 workmen have quit work at the camps." Then on May 3 a telegram went out from the IWW in the Okanagan to comrades in Spokane. It was on! "A strike has been declared on the Kettle Valley Construction work. All employment offices in cities of the Northwest must be picketed. Advise all men to stay away."[21]

What were the issues and what did the strike leaders expect? The *Industrial Worker* summarized: "We had no trouble getting the men off the line.... The demands are for a minimum wage of $3.00 per 10 hours for all men working on the grade; $50.00 a month for flunkeys and bull cooks; cooks, $90.00 a month. The present rate of wages on the line is $2.75 for 10 hours; $40 to $45 for car teamsters and the same for flunkeys and bull cooks." The article continued with a harangue, referencing Premier Richard McBride and the provincial police: "We expect McBride's Specials are already under orders.... It sure is a good thing that the I.W.W.s are passive resisters, for if they showed the least sign of being otherwise, McBride would be minus a very large number of his noble upholders."[22]

Both sides in the strike prepared for action. The Wobbly organizers acquired an old sawmill in Naramata and converted it into a large bunkhouse, bringing in provisions and preparing meals. They arranged for their own police to keep the peace and especially deal with any who consumed liquor "not wisely but too well." For its part the authorities sent a squad of provincial police to "keep order," rushing in three regular and twelve special constables. The contractors, after calling the leaders "agitators," and their entourage, members of the "hobo" class, brought in a number of strike breakers.[23]

Depending upon which account one reads, the number of men on strike ranged from 400 to 1,000. Although the numbers varied, what clearly emerged was that the work on the east side of the lake suffered serious disruption for over a week. Although stiffs on the Summerland side did not stop work, supposedly they had better conditions, the strikers tied up the line from Kelowna to Penticton, nearly 47 miles in all.

Most reports imply that the strike did not affect the men in Myra Canyon, although that may be because the issues there had already been resolved. Testimony before the touring Commission on Labour declared that a walk-out had occurred earlier over money. George Chew, the main contractor, had responded by raising wages from $2.75 per day to $3.00, precisely the figure at the heart of the strike. There was no need for job action there.[24]

The local IWW may have contemplated a long strike like that against the Canadian Northern in 1912, but it did not last long. Within a week, a fortnight at most, all the men returned to work or had been replaced. According to supporters of the contractors, the disruption collapsed because of the prompt and firm action of the provincial police in keeping the strikers away from the grade. That plus the clear intention of the authorities to repress disorder with a firm hand had limited it. A more likely explanation was that many of the men who laid down their tools were not really enthusiastic about the action. Navvies were notoriously mobile and some left the valley in search of other work, thus depleting the IWW numbers. Others, needing their wages, returned to work, probably remembering the lack of IWW success the year before with its strike against the Canadian Northern. Further, it did not help that other unions expressed hostility toward the Wobblies and offered no assistance, neither in resources nor moral support.[25] For example, the *British Columbia Federationist*, the organ of the craft unions, wrote caustically: "The didactics of these propagandists are largely sophistical buncombe," a polite way of saying the IWW supporters were pieces of excrement! The Wobblies attempted to put the best face forward, announcing the gain of some small concessions, then adding, the "difficulty regarding the establishment of a commissary necessitated a return to the grade."[26]

Unfortunately for the stiff, the IWW had again failed to improve his lot. Wages remained at $2.75 per day and little had changed, other than to intensify the anger of employers towards the union. But did the strike have any impact other than to reduce the credibility of the Wobblies? Warren, the president of the KVR, later claimed that it had had a significant impact on subcontractors. After 1914 when these men prepared to sue Grant Smith for extra compensation, they claimed they had lost money because of changes in the planned line. Warren argued instead that they lost money because of the intermittent labour problems which culminated in the strike and it had taken them some time to recover financially.[27]

Life and leisure on the grade and in the camps had moments of excitement, periods of escape, occasions of profit and situations of pleasure. There were even times of hope, gratitude and anticipation. For this the stiff might thank first those who provided him with physical delight, the liquor merchant, the prostitute and the card shark. Later in a more contemplative moment the stiff might express gratitude to the others who cared about more than his fleeting amusements, the social reformer, the Christian, the Marxist and the humanitarian. These folks represented the good people who fretted about his well being. But the stiff also faced other moments associated with loss, pain, hopelessness or despair. Consider the itinerant who lost all his wages at cards, suffered the excruciating pain of an injury, felt hopeless after weeks of hard work with only pennies to show or despaired of ever making enough to acquire his homestead. All these emotions were found in the camps and with the stiffs. Working on the railway, working on the KVR, working anywhere as a stiff had its regular pains, its intermittent pleasures, its infrequent rewards and its patchy profits. The men might ask if it was a good or a miserable life. It depended upon the stiff but he probably said it was just a tough life.

[1] "Young Italian Frozen to Death," *Kelowna Courier,* March 20, 1913, 7.

[2] "Police Court," *Kelowna Courier,* March 27, 1913, 6.

[3] "Illicit Liquor Selling in the Railway Camps," *Orchard City Record*, May 14, 1914, 8.

[4] "K.V.R. in Naramata," *Summerland Review,* September 27, 1912, 1.

[5] "Naramata News," *Industrial Worker,* March 13, 1913, 1.

[6] Ted Logie, *Ted Tells (Okanagan) Tales* (Summerland: Summerland Museum Archivist Group, 1968), 170.

[7] "Police Raid Italian Gambling Den," *Orchard City Record,* November 30, 1913, 1.

[8] "Railroad Engineers Entertain Friends at Dance," *Orchard City Record,* April 9, 1914, 6. The engineers included Messrs. G. W. Buck, G. G. Gladman, A. R. Moore and J. C. Denkel. Grant Smith was represented by Messrs. A. W. Henning, K. D. Hauser, H. H. Cloutier, G. S. Harmount, G. L. Ekstrom, C. N. Martin and E. H. Johnson.

[9] "Our Naramata Section," *Summerland Review,* December 5, 1913, 6.

[10] "Basketball," *Penticton Herald,* February 7, 1914, 6.

[11] Jean Burnet, "An Introduction," in Bradwin, xiii-xiv.

[12] "News from the Railroad Camps," *Summerland Review,* January 31, 1913, 1.

[13] "Railway Camp Work," *Summerland Review,* December 6, 1912, 3.

[14] "History of Transportation Department," YMCA Archives, Anderson Library, University of Minnesota, www.special.lib.umn.edu/findaid/html/ymca; "Penticton," *Vernon News,* August 14, 1913, 8. See also "Penticton," *Vernon News,* August 28, 1913, 6.

[15] "W.C.T.U. Holds Annual Meeting," *Orchard City Record,* May 21, 1914, 7. See also "Mission Work Amongst the Foreigners," *Orchard City Record,* June 12, 1913, 3.

[16] McCormack, 5.

[17] Ibid.

[18] "Police Persecution Near Naramata, BC," *Industrial Worker,* March 6, 1913, 1.

[19] "IWW's at Work," *Penticton Herald,* February 15, 1913, 4.

[20] "Thorne Gets Thirty Days," *Industrial Worker,* February 27, 1913, 1; "Naramata," *Vernon News,* March 27, 1913, 6; "The Labour Situation on the K.V.R.R. Construction," *Kelowna Courier,* May 15, 1913, 1.

[21] "I.W.W.," *The Ledge,* March 13, 1913, 4; "Strike of Workers at Construction Camps," *Penticton Herald,* March 29, 1913, 1; "Naramata," *Vernon News,* April 17, 1913, 6; "Stay Away from Naramata," *Industrial Worker,* May 8, 1913, 1.

[22] "Strike Is Off in Naramata," *Industrial Worker,* May 15, 1913, 1.

[23] "Laborers Strike on Kettle Valley Line," *Vernon News,* May 8, 1913, 1; "Strike Fizzels Out," *Vernon News,* May 15, 1913, 4; "The Labour Situation on the K.V.R.R. Construction."

[24] "The Labour Situation on the K.V.R.R. Construction."

[25] "I.W.W. Strike at Naramata; Not the Success Anticipated by Organizers," *Summerland Review,* May 9, 1913, 1; "Strike Fizzels Out"; "Kettle Valley Strikers Returning to Work," *Daily News,* May 13, 1913, 1.

[26] "The American Labor Movement and Disruptionist Policy of I.W.W.," *British Columbia Federationist,* April 18, 1913, 1; "Strike Is Off in Naramata."

[27] Warren to Shaughnessy, Trail, BC, March 12, 1917, CPA

CONCLUSION

This most unusual of Canadian railways has left us with a bountiful collection of stories. It did not follow the usual route of valleys, river banks and reasonably level ground, but went up and over the hills and mountains, not once, but three times. It did not pass through bustling or well established communities or connect major centres, but journeyed through sparsely inhabited regions where population centres numbered in the several hundreds or perhaps a few thousands. It employed one of North America's great civil engineers who conquered some near-impossible terrain. It boasted a team that built one of the longest and highest bridges of its kind at Trout Creek. It claimed a master planner who accomplished one of the great engineering feats in the Quintette Tunnels. It included a stretch which negotiated the tricky hillside of Myra Canyon, leaving a legacy of one of the country's most spectacular six mile segments of rail bed.

Its stories continued with the challenge of maintenance, the anxiety of passage and the anomaly of names. Not all railways dealt regularly with 150 or 200 feet of snow in order to keep parts of its route open in the winter. Not many other lines had a safety record where no paying passenger ever perished while riding its trains. Not all railways had sections where passengers closed their eyes or avoided looking out because of acrophobia. Not many sojourners passed by or through Shakespearean place names like Romeo, Juliet, Iago, Lear or Othello in order to arrive at their destination.

These reminders represent well-known stories. Now there is another story, the tale of the Naramata navvy, the Sawmill stiff and the Myra moiler, all labouring to build the KVR. These Italians from Naples, Austrians from Habsburg Galicia, Russians arriving from Vladivostok and Swedes fresh from Stockholm came, laboured and conquered the terrain. Most of their names have escaped us since there was not much need to know them as long as they swung their picks, scooped their shovels and filled their wheelbarrows. Yet they were vital to the line and especially crucial to the Okanagan valley. For all the well earned credit we give to McCulloch, Warren, Shaughnessy and company, the real credit was quite simple: no stiff, no railway. True, Grant Smith exploited them, Morrissey paid them minimally, the BC government generally ignored them and the respectable citizens of Kelowna and Penticton viewed them with some trepidation. But they had their stories which deserve a more prominent place in railway annals. They worked up a mighty sweat on the grade. They ran like hell after setting the explosive charges. They sought the forgetfulness induced by liquor. They enjoyed the comradery of fellow countrymen in a strange land. They trudged to town to send money home or to look for other enjoyments. They were often homesick. Like their counterparts on other rail lines, the Okanagan stiffs gave their sweat, tears, blood and occasionally their lives to help develop this land. That was no small accomplishment. They deserve to be honoured through a collective memory of who they were, what they did and how they lived. Our journey with Myra's men sets us out on that path.

AFTERWORD:

MYRA CANYON
AFTER THE KVR AND THE CPR

The last CPR train to pass through Myra Canyon was in May 1973. After that date the abandoned line began to fall into disrepair although it attracted a number of recreationalists who either hiked or used their automobiles on the rails. Some Okanagan residents, reluctant to see the railway completely abandoned, lobbied various levels of government to preserve the tracks and operate the line in the McCulloch Lake area, including Myra Canyon, as a tourist attraction. They formed the Kettle Valley Rail Heritage Society. Unfortunately, their efforts were not successful and in 1980 the CPR removed the tracks, ties and telegraph poles, leaving only the rail bed.[1]

Although at that time no plan existed for use of the Myra Canyon corridor, local people began to frequent the right-of-way and the trestles for walking and cycling. On some occasions local school children hiked the rail bed from McCulloch Lake, through Myra Canyon and on to Bellevue Creek as part of their outdoor science and history programmes. Vandalism and neglect, however, meant the trestles and tunnels deteriorated and became dangerous. After two incidents in which cyclists fell off the trestles and suffered serious injuries, the provincial government considered closing the route to the public.

In 1993 a small group, mainly residents of Kelowna, formed the Myra Canyon Trestle Restoration Society (MCTRS). They planned to lay boardwalks and erect guardrails on each of the eighteen trestles to make them safer for the public. Although none of the volunteers in this group had had experience with bridges or had more than a passing knowledge of railways, they entered the work with great enthusiasm and energy. Over the next two years, with generous support from individuals, the business community and the public, they completed the rehabilitation of all eighteen trestles.

One part of their work which has generated some comment concerns the numbering of the Myra Canyon trestles. When the MCTRS volunteers began, they were not familiar with the tradition of measuring railway distances from east to west. Since the group launched its work on the western most trestle in the canyon, the volunteers designated it as trestle 1 and then proceeded to work eastward. Consequently the numbering system, in railway lingo, is backwards – but so it remains.

Following the "grand opening" of the rehabilitated trestles in 1995, MCTRS continued its involvement with the area. It undertook the maintenance of the trail, erected benches, toilets and interpretive signs and built a portal cribbing structure in one of the tunnels. Its on-going work also included rock scaling to ensure trail safety and brush-clearing to keep the rail bed free from overgrown vegetation. In 1998 the society installed electronic counters which quickly confirmed the increased usage by the public. The 26,600 annual visitors of 1998 rose to 50,000 just before the devastating 2003 fire.

Since members of MCTRS had worked in the canyon on a regular basis, they recognized the special attributes of the area and began lobbying to protect Myra Canyon and environs with park status. After five years of efforts through the Okanagan Shuswap Land and Resource Management Plan (OSLRMP), in 2000 the BC government established the Myra-Bellevue Provincial Park with Myra Canyon as a primary feature. Two other designations soon followed, also enhancing the reputation and affirming the uniqueness of this area. First, the sponsors of the TransCanada Trail decided to use the KVR right-of-way as their route through the southern interior of British Columbia. Then in January 2003, just two years after MCTRS applied for the designation, the Myra Canyon section of the Kettle Valley Railway received the status as a National Historic Site.

In August 2003 the Okanagan Mountain Park fire ravaged the canyon, destroying twelve of the sixteen wooden trestles plus the wooden superstructures of the two steel ones. The loss of these historic features became national and international news with coverage as far away as Australia, Germany and the United Kingdom. Although the loss was devastating, the MCTRS directors immediately affirmed that the trestles would be rebuilt. Gordon Campbell, the Premier of British Columbia, agreed and appointed a four person task force, representing the federal, provincial and local governments as well as MCTRS, with responsibility to develop a restoration plan. This group recommended not just the rebuilding of the trestles, but rebuilding them to resemble the originals to preserve the outstanding heritage and recreational values of this remarkable railway.

Thanks to support from both politicians and officials in Ottawa and Victoria, the federal/provincial disaster relief fund paid for the cost of rebuilding. This fund, derived from a standing agreement between each province and the federal government, specifies that the federal government pays 90 per cent of eligible costs and the province, 10 per cent.

On June 22, 2008, the Myra Canyon trestles officially re-opened with a grand celebration. Members of the public and visitors from across Canada and the world once more walked, hiked and cycled this historic route. The Kettle Valley Railway, once the dream which became reality, was again transformed, this time, not as a guarantee of sovereignty or as an engine of economic development, but as a reminder of a distant era and as a monument to an outstanding historical and recreational site.

---

[1] Many thanks to Ken and Gwen Campbell of MCTRS for providing much of the information in this Afterword.

ACKNOWLEDGEMENTS

Many people and organizations helped make this book a reality. The Myra Canyon Trestle Restoration Society provided generous funding to conduct the research. Then the Society's role as publisher was invaluable. I am deeply grateful for their encouragement and support.

My friend and colleague, Richard Garvin and I began this project in 2006 when we embarked on an historical-archaeological study of the original work camps in Myra Canyon. Rick, who is an archaeologist, introduced me to the wonders and joys of archaeology as we conducted our first "dig" with students in the summer of 2007. I appreciate his balanced and steadfast support on this part of our joint project.

Barrie Sanford, the author of *McCulloch's Wonder,* went out of his way to help with information, resources, materials and advice. His knowledge and love of the KVR and Canadian railways were always present during our many conversations. Joe Smuin, author of *Kettle Valley Railway Mileboards,* also gave his time and expertise to help complete this project. Thanks also to Joe for suggesting the book title.

During my work in various archives I met some wonderful and extremely helpful people. Peter Ord and Jeanne Boyle at the Penticton Museum and Archives deserve a very special thank you. They gave me easy access to all their KVR materials (Penticton is the main repository for the KVR), they loaned maps, they provided a photocopier, they generously allowed me to use their many photographs and they always made me feel welcome. In Montreal at the CPR archives Bob Kennell and Jo-Anne Colby were especially helpful. Their discovery of the Warren/Shaughnessey correspondence just weeks before I arrived was not only timely, it was crucial to this book. They were also exceptionally generous with photocopying, the indispensable tool for all researchers today. Wayne Wilson and his colleagues at the Kelowna museums provided newspapers and records for the Central Okanagan perspective on the KVR. Finally, Sherril Foster at the Summerland Museum, Jane Davey at the Northwest Museum in Spokane, Washington, the several archivists in Victoria at the Provincial Archives, as well as the curators in Greenwood, Midway and Vernon deserve another special thanks.

My colleagues and friends at the University of British Columbia Okanagan, James Hull, Eric Nellis and Duane Thomson, gave me timely, insightful and crucial advice. Their suggestions and counsel have guided me through the joys and tribulations of writing and editing a book. Duane especially helped me through some of the "rough spots" of the manuscript and assisted with a great deal of the proofreading. I also appreciate the several suggestions which came from other readers – Ken Campbell of the MCTRS who has adopted the KVR as his special project and to whom many owe a debt as the chief promoter to rebuild the trestles after the 2003 fire, and to Randy Manuel of Penticton, one of the original preservers of the KVR heritage. Thank you also goes to several other readers for their timely and valuable comments: Shannon Baudais, Graham Bruce, Hans and Josine Kruiswyk, Carol Thomson and Judie Steeves.

I particularly want to thank Ashley Black, my student research assistant. Ashley worked on the various engineers' reports in order to compile the lists, technical details and information for the Appendices. Her contribution was invaluable and I owe her a deep debt of gratitude.

A special thank you also goes to Donna Szelest who designed the cover and laid out the text and photographs. Donna's help was significant on the many technical details. Nancy Wise of Sandhill Book Marketing also gave other valuable technical assistance and suggestions, and guided me through many of the intricacies of preparing a book for publication. Nancy too deserves many thanks.

Finally, I wish to acknowledge the special help from my wife Linda. Not only did she assist with the research and accumulate materials on Myra's men, she allowed me to close the door to my study and work uninterruptedly. Without her support and understanding, this book would not now be published. Thanks is never enough for the friend and companion who supports you, but thank you, Linda.

SOURCES AND SELECTED BIBLIOGRAPHY

I. SOURCE MATERIALS USED IN THE TEXT

A. ARCHIVES

Barrie Sanford Archives & the Andrew McCulloch Foundation, Brookmere, BC

    KVR materials

    Photographs

British Columbia Archives, Victoria

    BC *Sessional Papers*, 1912, 1913, 1914, 1915

    GR0446, Provincial Game Warden

    GR0684, BC Commission on Labour

    GR0799, BC Commission on the Pacific Great Eastern Railway

    GR0956, Ministry of Forests, Vernon

Canadian Pacific Archives, Montreal, Quebec

    KVR, RG2.92934, folders 1 – 10

    Miscellaneous KVR files

Greenwood Archives, Greenwood, BC

    Greenwood Transportation files

Kelowna Museum and Archives, Kelowna, BC

    Newspapers

    Photographic collection

Midway Archives, Midway, BC

    KVR files

Northwest Museum of Arts and Culture, Joel E. Ferris Research Library and Archives, Spokane, Washington

    W. S. Mortimer photographic collection

    Miscellaneous railroad files

Penticton Museum and Archives, Penticton, BC

    KVR Fonds

    Photograph collections: Lois Cuenin, KVR, Joy Morgan, Maclod, Bill Moon, R. A. Welford

Robert Abbey, private collection, Penticton, BC

    Andrew McCulloch's field diaries

Summerland Museum and Archives, Summerland, BC

    KVR binder and files

Vernon Museum and Archives, Vernon, BC

    Photograph collection

B. NEWSPAPERS AND JOURNALS

Annual Reports of the Okanagan Historical Society,
1948, 1949, 1966, 1979

Boundary Historical Society Reports, 1964, 1967

British Columbia Federationist (Vancouver), 1911 - 1914

Canadian Railway and Marine World, 1910 - 1915

Daily News (Nelson), 1911 - 1914

Grand Forks Gazette, 1911 - 1914

Industrial Worker (Spokane), 1912 - 1914

Kelowna Courier and Okanagan Orchardist, 1910 - 1915

The Ledge (Greenwood), 1910 - 1914

Penticton Herald, 1911 - 1917

Orchard City Record (Kelowna), 1910 - 1914

Summerland Review, 1910 - 1914

Vernon News, 1910 -1915

II. BOOKS AND PERIODICALS

Avery, Donald. *"Dangerous Foreigners"; European Immigrant Workers and Labour Radicalism in Canada, 1896 - 1932.* Toronto: McClelland and Stewart, 1979

Bradwin, Edmund. *The Bunkhouse Man; A Study of Work and Pay in the Camps of Canada, 1903 - 1914.* New York, 1928. Reprint Toronto: University of Toronto Press, 1972.

Burrows, Roger. *Railway Mileposts: British Columbia.* Vol. 1: *The CPR Mainline Route from the Rockies to the Pacific including the Okanagan Routes and CN's Canyon Route.* Vol. 2: *The Southern Routes from the Crowsnest to the Coquihalla including the Great Northern and Kettle Valley Routes.* North Vancouver: Railway Milepost Books, 1981, 1984.

Doeksen, Gerry. *Kettle Valley Railway.* Montros, BC: Gerry Doeksen, 1995.

Emmott, N. D. "Policing the Rails." *Canada West,* XXXI – XXXIII (1979), 14 -20.

Hill, Beth. *Exploring the Kettle Valley Railway.* Winlaw, BC: Polestar Book Publishers, 1989.

Logie, Ted. *Ted Tells (Okanagan) Tales.* Summerland, BC: Summerland Museum Archivist Group, 1990.

McCormack, Ross. *The Blanketstiffs: Itinerant Railway Construction Workers, 1896 -1914.* Montreal: National Film Board, 1974.

Sanford, Barrie. *McCulloch's Wonder: The Story of the Kettle Valley Railway.* North Vancouver: Whitecap Books, 1977 and 2002.

_____. *Steel Rails and Iron Men: A pictorial history of the Kettle Valley Railway.* North Vancouver: Whitecap Books, 1990 and 2003.

Smuin, Joe. *Canadian Pacific's Kettle Valley Railway*. Calgary: British Railway Modellers of North America, 1997.

_____. *Kettle Valley Railway Mileboards: A Historical Field Guide to the KVR*. Winnipeg: North Kildonan Publications, 2003.

Turner, Robert. *Steam on the Kettle Valley, A Railway Heritage Remembered*. Victoria: Sono Nis Press, 1995.

III.VIDEO RECORDINGS

Around the Horn: The KVR Line, 1890 - 1989. Merritt: MCTV9, Merritt Cablevision, 1989.

The KVR [Midway to Penticton], in the series *Gold Trails and Ghost Towns*, No. 21. Kelowna: CHBC, 2000?.

The KVR [Boundary Country to Hope], in the series *Pioneers and Places*, No. 102. Kelowna: CHBC, 1999.

The KVR/Myra, in the series *Pioneers and Places*, No. 511. Kelowna: CHBC, 2003.

KVR East, in the series *Gold Trails and Ghost Towns*, No. 702. Kelowna: CHBC, 1993.

KVR West, in the series *Gold Trails and Ghost Towns*, No. 809. Kelowna: CHBC, 1995.

Myra Canyon Explorer; Trestles, Bridges and Tunnels of the Kettle Valley Ry. in and near Myra Canyon. Winfield, BC: LPD Publishing, 2003.

TRESTLES, TUNNELS & TRACKLAYING

KETTLE VALLEY RAILWAY
1913 -1914

Notes:

1. The mileage from Midway is according to Joe Smuin, *Kettle Valley Railway Mileboards*. The mileage from Hydraulic Summit was calculated by research assistant Ashley Black using the various engineers' reports.

2. Station numbers come from Andrew McCulloch's field diary, 1913. The mileage associated with the station numbers was calculated as "station number divided by 52.8."

3. Sources for all trestles, tunnels and tracklaying:

    McCulloch and Assistant Engineers reports, Penticton Museum & Archives Memoranda, J. J. Warren (President, KVR) to Thomas Shaughnessey (President, CPR).

    McCulloch's annual field diaries.

4. According to J. J. Warren, all trestles from mile 58 to 20 were completed by August 17, 1914.

5. There are occasional discrepancies between the mileage from Midway with the mileage from Hydraulic Summit, probably due to subsequent re-numberings.

A. CONSTRUCTION SCHEDULE FOR THE TRESTLES

1. From Hydraulic Summit

Trestle:	mile 76.3 from Midway, mile 1 from Hydraulic
	foundation began Sept 15-21, 1913
	assembly began Dec 7-14, 1913
	completed Dec 15-21, 1913
Trestle:	mile 77.8 from Midway, mile 2 from Hydraulic
	station 95 or mile 1.799
	foundation began Oct 15-21, 1913
	assembly began Dec 7-14, 1914
	completed Dec 15-21, 1914

2. Myra Canyon Trestles

Numbers refer to current Myra Canyon Trestle Restoration Society numbering system

Trestle 18: mile 84.9 from Midway, mile 8.9 from Hydraulic
foundation began Aug 1-7, 1913
assembly began Jan 6, 1914
completed Jan 8-14, 1914

Trestle 17: mile 85.2 from Midway, mile 9.2 from Hydraulic
foundation began Aug 1-7, 1913
assembly began Jan 8-14, 1914
completed Jan 8-14, 1914

Trestle 16: mile 85.25 from Midway, mile 9.25 from Hydraulic
foundation began Aug 1-7, 1913
assembly began Jan 8-14, 1914
completed Jan 15-21, 1914

Trestle 15: mile 85.3 from Midway, mile 9.3 from Hydraulic
station 494 or mile 9.356
foundation began Aug 1-7, 1913
assembly began Jan 15-21, 1914
completed Jan 22-31, 1914

Trestle 14: mile 85.35 from Midway, mile 9.35 from Hydraulic
station 496 or mile 9.393
foundations began Aug 1-7, 1913
assembly began Jan 22-31, 1914
completed Feb 1-7, 1914

Trestle 13: mile 85.45 from Midway, mile 9.45 from Hydraulic
station 498 or mile 9.431
foundations began Aug 1-7, 1913
assembly began Feb 1-7, 1914
completed Feb 8-14, 1914

Trestle 12: mile 85.6 from Midway, mile 9.6 from Hydraulic
foundations began Aug 1-7, 1913
assembly began Feb 8-14, 1914
completed Feb 15-21, 1914

Trestle 11: mile 85.9 from Midway, mile 9.9 from Hydraulic
foundations began Aug 1-7, 1913
assembly began Feb 15-21, 1914
completed Mar 17, 1914

Trestle 10: mile 86.4 from Midway, mile 10.4 from Hydraulic
assembly began Apr 8-14, 1914
completed Apr 8-14, 1914

Trestle 9: mile 86.5 from Midway, mile 10.5 from Hydraulic
KLO/East Fork Canyon Creek
foundations began Nov 1-7, 1913
assembly began Apr 15-21
completed May 15-21, 1914

Trestle 8: mile 86.55 from Midway, mile 10.55 from Hydraulic
station 562 or mile 10.568
foundations began Nov 1-7, 1913
assembly began Apr 21-30, 1914
completed May 21-31, 1914

Trestle: mile 86.9 from Midway, mile 10.9 from Hydraulic
assembly began May 22-31, 1914
completed May 22-31, 1914
gravel filled, 1928

Trestle 7: mile 87.4 from Midway, mile 11.5 from Hydraulic
foundations began Oct 1-7, 1913
assembly began May 22-31, 1914
completed June 1-7, 1914

Trestle 6: mile 87.9 from Midway, mile 11.9 from Hydraulic
Pooley/West Fork Canyon Creek
station 634 or mile 12.007
foundation began Sept 1-7, 1913
assembly began June 9, 1914
completed by July 10, 1914

Trestle 5: mile 88 from Midway, mile 12 from Hydraulic
further information unavailable

Trestle 4: mile 88.2 from Midway, mile 12.2 from Hydraulic
foundation began week of Sept 8-14, 1913
further information unavailable

Trestle 3: mile 88.4 from Midway, mile 12.4 from Hydraulic
built in June, 1928

Trestle: mile 88.6 from Midway, mile 12.6 from Hydraulic
foundation began Sept 8-14, 1913
assembly began June 15-21, 1914
completed by Sept 15, 1914
bypassed, 1946

Trestle 2: mile 89.4 from Midway, mile 13.4 from Hydraulic
assembly began June 1-7, 1914 (?)
completed Oct 2, 1914 – last spike on this trestle

Trestle 1: mile 90.4 from Midway, mile 14.77 from Hydraulic
station 778 or mile 14.734
assembly began Mar 23, 1914
completed ?

3. Beyond Myra Canyon toward Penticton

Trestle: mile 92.1 from Midway, mile 16.1 from Hydraulic
East Fork Priest Creek
assembly began Apr 22-30, 1914
completed May 1-7, 1914
gravel filled, 1944

Trestle: mile 93.2 from Midway, mile 17 from Hydraulic
West Fork Priest Creek
station 872 or mile 16.515
assembly began Jan 8-14, 1914
completed May 1-7, 1914
gravel filled, 1944?

Trestle: mile 95.5 from Midway, mile 19.5
assembly began Apr 28, 1914
completed May 1-7, 1914
gravel filled, 1945

Trestle: mile 95.8 from Midway, mile 19.8 from Hydraulic
assembly began April 7, 1914
completed ?
gravel filled, 1947

Trestle: mile 96.3 from Midway, mile 20.3 from Hydraulic
East Fork Sawmill/Bellevue Creek
station 1057 or mile 20.018
foundation began Nov 15-21, 1913
further information unavailable

Trestle: mile 98.6 from Midway, mile 22.7 from Hydraulic
West Fork Sawmill/Gillard Creek
foundation began Oct 8-14, 1913
assembly began Jun 13, 1914
not completed before Jul 10, 1914
bypassed, 1961

Trestles: between miles 98 – 110 from Midway, miles 22 – 34 from Hydraulic
7 trestles built between May 21-Jun 7, 1914

Trestle: mile 119.5 from Midway, mile 43.7 from Hydraulic
assembly began week of Mar 8-14, 1914
completed Mar 21-31, 1914
gravel filled, 1923

Trestle: mile 123.3 from Midway, mile 47.5 from Hydraulic
Mill Creek
assembly began Feb 21-28, 1914
completed Mar 1-7, 1914
gravel filled, 1924

Trestle: mile 125 from Midway, mile 49 from Hydraulic
Camp Creek
assembly began Feb 1-7, 1914
completed Feb 15-21, 1914
gravel filled, 1925

Trestle: mile 126.1 from Midway, mile 50.1 from Hydraulic
             no other information available
             gravel filled, 1920

Trestle: mile127.7 from Midway, mile 52 from Hydraulic
             assembly began Oct 15-21, 1913
             completed Nov 1-7, 1913
             gravel filled, 1923

Trestle: mile 128.9 from Midway, mile 53 from Hydraulic
             assembly began Sept 15-21, 1913
             completed Oct 15-21, 1913
             gravel filled, 1921

Trestle: mile 130.2 from Midway, mile 54.4 from Hydraulic
             assembly began before Aug 21-31, 1913
             completed Sept 21-30, 1913
             gravel filled, 1920

Trestle: mile 132.6 from Midway, mile 56 from Hydraulic
             Penticton Creek
             assembly began Aug 1-7, 1913
             completed ?

B. TUNNELS – MYRA CANYON TO PENTICTON

Tunnel: mile 84.7 from Midway, mile 8.95 from Hydraulic
station 472 or mile 8.939
began east portal, Jan 12, 1913
began west portal, Apr 10, 1913
Jul 12, 1913, McCulloch decided to cut out the top and
make a rock cut

Tunnel: mile 85.7 from Midway, mile 9.85 from Hydraulic
station 522 or mile 9.886
began prior to Jun 21, 1913
completed Jul 14-21, 1913

Tunnel: mile 86.2 from Midway, mile 10.46 from Hydraulic
station 557 or mile 10.549
began prior to Jun 7, 1913
completed Aug 1-7, 1913

Tunnel: mile 113.9 from Midway, mile 38 from Hydraulic
Adra or Big Tunnel
began prior to Jan 17, 1913
completed week of May 8-14, 1914

Tunnel: mile 120 from Midway, mile 45 from Hydraulic
Naramata or Little Tunnel
station 2391 or mile 45.28
began prior to Feb 1913
completed before Dec 20, 1913

C. TRACKLAYING

Note: Most of this information comes from the Assistant Engineers' reports, although these records end in June 1914, leaving no specific coverage of progress between miles 11.9 (West Fork Canyon or Pooley Creek trestle) and mile 22 (Sawmill or Gillard Creek trestle). J. J. Warren's memoranda, however, help complete the record.

READ
DOWN

Miles 0-1.5 completed by Dec 21, 1913

Up to 7 by Dec 31, 1913
Up to 9 by Jan 7, 1914
Up to 9.13 by Jan 7, 1914
Up to 9.2 by Jan 14, 1914 (to trestle 17)
Up to 9.3 by Jan 31, 1914 (to trestle 15)
Up to 9.5 by Feb 7, 1914 (just past trestle 13)
Up to 9.6 by Feb 14, 1914 (to trestle 12)
Up to 9.75 by Feb 21, 1914 (between trestles 12 & 11)
Up to 10.3 by Apr 14, 1914 (between trestles 11 & 10)
Up to 10.5 by Apr 21, 1914 (to trestle 9)
Up to 11.5 by May 31, 1914 (to trestle 7)
Up to 11.9 by Jun 7, 1914 (to trestle 6)
Up to 12.4 by Sept 15, 1914 (to bypassed trestle)

Last tracklaying, Friday, October 2, 1914.

Up to 14.4 by Sept 19, 1914
Up to 19.7 by Sept 15, 1914
Up to 20 by Aug 17, 1914
Up to 22.7 by Jun 7, 1914
Up to 30 by May 31, 1914
Up to 34 by May 21, 1914
Up to 38.5 by Mar 31, 1914 (Adra Tunnel)
Up to 43.7 by Mar 14, 1914
Up to 47.5 by Feb 28, 1914
Up to 48 by Feb 21, 1914

READ
UP

Up to 49 by Jan 31, 1914
From mile 58 to 54.5 by Jan 21, 1914

MEN ON THE WORK SITE
MYRA CANYON
1913

Date	Mile	7 - 8	8 - 9	9 - 10	10 - 11	11 - 12	12 - 13	13 - 14	14 - 15	TOTAL
June 1 - 7	Foremen	2	1	0	5	0	4	2	4	18
	Men	48	24	60	87	45	42	14	53	373
	Horses	3	2	3	5	3	3	1	5	25
	Cars	8	7	8	16	8	10	2	7	66
June 8 - 14	Foremen	2	2	0	5	0	4	2	4	19
	Men	47	45	49	95	45	48	14	46	389
	Horses	3	3	3	6	3	4	1	5	28
	Cars	8	7	8	15	9	10	3	10	70
June 15 - 21	Foremen	3	2	0	5	0	4	3	4	21
	Men	49	46	54	92	41	48	28	42	400
	Horses	4	3	3	6	3	4	0	3	26
	Cars	10	7	8	15	9	10	4	7	70
June 22 - 30	Foremen	3	2	0	7	0	4	2	4	22
	Men	47	48	57	90	29	46	28	53	398
	Horses	2	3	3	7	2	4	1	5	27
	Cars	6	6	7	15	5	6	6	10	61
July 1 - 7	Foremen	3	1	0	6	0	4	3	4	21
	Men	50	16	37	100	27	43	27	46	346
	Horses	3	1	3	9	2	3	3	3	27
	Cars	6	5	6	15	6	6	6	7	57
July 8 - 14	Foremen	3	1	0	6	0	4	3	3	20
	Men	38	9	20	100	27	42	30	39	305
	Horses	3	1	2	10	2	3	3	3	27
	Cars	6	2	5	15	6	6	7	8	55
July 15 - 21	Foremen	2	1	1	6	0	4	3	2	19
	Men	19	12	14	96	29	35	30	22	257
	Horses	1	1	1	7	3	3	3	5	24
	Cars	4	2	3	15	7	6	7	5	49
July 22 - 31	Foremen	3	1	1	6	0	0	3	2	16
	Men	33	24	9	76	27	0	25	17	211
	Horses	4	3	0	5	4	0	3	2	21
	Cars	8	6	2	15	7	0	7	3	48
Aug 1 - 7	Foremen	3	2	1	7	0	0	3	2	18
	Men	28	30	4	74	25	0	27	31	219
	Horses	4	2	0	5	4	0	3	4	22
	Cars	8	6	0	15	7	0	5	6	47

Date	Mile	7 - 8	8 - 9	9 - 10	10 - 11	11 - 12	12 - 13	13 - 14	14 - 15	TOTAL
Aug 8 - 14	Foremen	2	1	2	6	0	2	2	3	18
	Men	23	31	11	54	24	19	20	31	213
	Horses	0	2	0	5	4	2	2	2	17
	Cars	4	6	0	15	7	6	5	7	50
Aug 15 - 21	Foremen	2	1	2	6	0	2	2	2	17
	Men	25	30	11	52	20	20	20	28	206
	Horses	2	3	0	5	3	2	2	3	20
	Cars	6	7	0	15	7	6	4	7	52
Aug 22 - 31	Foremen	2	2	2	4	0	2	3	4	19
	Men	23	28	11	38	18	21	24	43	206
	Horses	1	3	0	4	3	2	1	3	17
	Cars	5	7	0	15	6	6	5	7	51
Sept 1 - 7	Foremen	1	2	2	7	0	2	3	3	20
	Men	8	21	12	56	23	21	31	30	202
	Horses	1	2	0	7	3	1	3	2	19
	Cars	2	7	0	15	6	6	7	4	47
Sept 8 - 14	Foremen	1	1	1	8	0	2	2	3	18
	Men	8	23	9	66	20	21	32	41	220
	Horses	1	2	0	7	3	2	2	4	21
	Cars	2	7	0	15	6	6	5	8	49
Sept 15 - 21	Foremen	1	1	1	7	0	2	3	4	19
	Men	6	23	8	62	19	27	25	31	201
	Horses	1	3	0	7	3	2	3	4	23
	Cars	2	6	0	16	6	6	7	8	51
Sept 22 - 30	Foremen	1	1	1	7	0	3	3	3	19
	Men	6	23	8	60	18	30	22	28	195
	Horses	1	3	0	7	3	2	3	3	22
	Cars	2	6	0	16	6	6	6	6	48
Oct 1 - 7	Foremen	1	1	1	7	0	3	1	3	17
	Men	6	18	16	63	18	33	10	26	190
	Horses	1	2	1	7	2	3	1	3	20
	Cars	2	4	2	16	6	7	2	7	46
Oct 8 - 14	Foremen	0	0	2	8	0	3	3	3	19
	Men	0	18	18	63	15	49	25	27	215
	Horses	0	2	1	7	2	3	3	4	22
	Cars	0	4	2	14	6	7	6	6	45
Oct 15 - 21	Foremen	0	0	1	8	1	3	3	4	20
	Men	0	18	17	63	25	52	24	33	232
	Horses	0	2	1	7	3	2	2	5	22
	Cars	0	4	2	14	6	6	6	8	46

MEN ON THE WORK SITE MYRA CANYON 1913

Date	Mile	7 - 8	8 - 9	9 - 10	10 - 11	11 - 12	12 - 13	13 - 14	14 - 15	TOTAL
Oct 22 - 31	Foremen	0	0	1	8	4	3	1	4	21
	Men	0	18	7	66	47	40	10	43	231
	Horses	0	2	0	7	3	2	1	4	19
	Cars	0	4	0	14	6	6	2	9	41
Nov 1 - 7	Foremen	0	0	1	7	3	3	2	4	20
	Men	0	18	8	56	34	41	22	40	219
	Horses	0	2	0	7	3	2	1	3	18
	Cars	0	4	0	14	6	5	4	6	39
Nov 8 - 14	Foremen	0	0	1	8	4	2	2	4	21
	Men	0	18	8	72	48	37	17	34	234
	Horses	0	2	0	7	3	2	1	3	18
	Cars	0	4	0	14	6	6	2	5	37
Nov 15 - 21	Foremen	0	0	1	7	4	2	2	4	20
	Men	0	18	10	71	49	45	20	45	258
	Horses	0	2	0	7	3	1	1	4	18
	Cars	0	4	0	14	6	4	2	7	37
Nov 22 - 30	Foremen	0	0	1	7	4	2	2	5	21
	Men	0	18	10	62	54	34	21	46	245
	Horses	0	2	0	6	3	1	1	4	17
	Cars	0	4	0	14	6	4	2	8	38
Dec 1 - 7	Foremen	0	0	1	7	4	2	1	3	18
	Men	0	18	22	59	50	42	13	31	235
	Horses	0	2	0	6	3	2	1	2	16
	Cars	0	4	0	14	6	4	2	4	34
Dec 8 - 14	Foremen	0	0	1	7	3	2	no data	no data	13
	Men	0	16	18	66	43	28	no data	no data	171
	Horses	0	2	0	6	3	2	no data	no data	13
	Cars	0	4	0	14	6	4	no data	no data	28
Dec 15 - 21	Foremen	0	0	1	7	3	2	1	3	17
	Men	0	24	15	63	41	32	10	18	203
	Horses	0	3	0	6	3	2	1	2	17
	Cars	0	4	0	14	6	4	2	3	33
Dec 22 - 31	Foremen	1	0	0	7	3	2	1	1	15
	Men	4	21	4	61	41	24	6	7	168
	Horses	0	3	0	6	3	2	1	2	17
	Cars	0	4	0	14	6	4	2	3	33

MEN ON THE WORK SITE
MYRA CANYON
1914

Date	Mile	7 - 8	8 - 9	9 - 10	10 - 11	11 - 12	12 - 13	13 - 14	14 - 15	TOTAL
Jan 1 - 7	Foremen	0	0	1	4	2	1	1	0	9
	Men	0	16	17	47	32	21	5	0	138
	Horses	0	1	1	7	2	2	1	0	14
	Cars	0	4	0	10	4	3	2	0	23
Jan 8 - 14	Foremen	no data	0	1	7	2	2	0	1	13
	Men	no data	0	28	65	34	20	0	4	151
	Horses	no data	0	2	7	2	2	0	0	13
	Cars	no data	0	0	10	4	3	0	0	17
Jan 15 - 21	Foremen	no data	0	1	7	2	3	0	0	13
	Men	no data	0	28	66	33	30	0	0	157
	Horses	no data	0	2	7	2	2	0	0	13
	Cars	no data	0	0	10	4	3	0	0	17
Jan 22 - 31	Foremen	no data	0	1	6	2	2	0	0	11
	Men	no data	0	20	66	32	25	0	0	143
	Horses	no data	0	2	8	2	2	0	0	14
	Cars	no data	0	0	10	4	3	0	0	17
Feb 1 - 7	Foremen	no data	0	1	6	2	2	0	0	11
	Men	no data	0	22	78	34	25	0	0	159
	Horses	no data	0	2	9	2	2	0	0	15
	Cars	no data	0	0	10	4	3	0	0	17
Feb 8 - 14	Foremen	no data	0	1	7	2	2	0	0	12
	Men	no data	0	21	78	32	24	0	0	155
	Horses	no data	0	2	9	2	2	0	0	15
	Cars	no data	0	0	10	4	3	0	0	17
Feb 15 - 21	Foremen	no data	0	1	7	2	3	0	0	13
	Men	no data	0	21	72	32	29	0	0	154
	Horses	no data	0	2	9	2	2	0	0	15
	Cars	no data	0	0	10	4	3	0	0	17
Feb 22 - 28	Foremen	no data	0	0	9	2	3	0	0	14
	Men	no data	0	0	84	32	25	0	0	141
	Horses	no data	0	0	10	2	2	0	0	14
	Cars	no data	0	0	10	4	3	0	0	17
Mar 1 - 7	Foremen	no data	0	0	8	2	3	0	0	13
	Men	no data	0	0	76	35	27	0	0	138
	Horses	no data	0	0	11	2	2	0	0	15
	Cars	no data	0	0	10	4	3	0	0	17

MEN ON THE WORK SITE MYRA CANYON 1914

Date	Mile	7 - 8	8 - 9	9 - 10	10 - 11	11 - 12	12 - 13	13 - 14	14 - 15	TOTAL
Mar 8 - 14	Foremen	no data	0	0	7	2	3	0	0	12
	Men	no data	0	0	72	36	27	0	0	135
	Horses	no data	0	0	11	2	2	0	0	15
	Cars	no data	0	0	6	6	3	0	0	15
Mar 15 - 21	Foremen	no data	0	0	7	2	0	0	0	9
	Men	no data	0	0	64	34	0	0	0	98
	Horses	no data	0	0	11	2	0	0	0	13
	Cars	no data	0	0	6	6	0	0	0	12
Mar 22 - 31	Foremen	no data	1	0	6	2	0	0	1	10
	Men	no data	6	0	42	33	0	0	7	88
	Horses	no data	1	0	8	2	0	0	2	13
	Cars	no data	0	0	4	5	0	0	0	9
Apr 1 - 7	Foremen	no data	2	0	2	0	0	0	0	4
	Men	no data	25	0	28	0	0	0	0	53
	Horses	no data	2	0	2	0	0	0	0	4
	Cars	no data	0	0	4	0	0	0	0	4
Apr 8 - 14	Foremen	no data	1	0	2	1	0	0	0	4
	Men	no data	8	0	22	12	0	0	0	42
	Horses	no data	2	0	2	0	0	0	0	4
	Cars	no data	0	0	3	0	0	0	0	3
Apr 15 - 21	Foremen	no data	1	0	2	1	0	0	0	4
	Men	no data	8	0	23	12	0	0	0	43
	Horses	no data	2	0	2	0	0	0	0	4
	Cars	no data	0	0	3	0	0	0	0	3
Apr 22 - 30	Foremen	no data	1	0	1	2	3	0	0	7
	Men	no data	4	0	14	27	23	0	0	68
	Horses	no data	0	0	1	3	4	0	0	8
	Cars	no data	0	0	2	0	2	0	0	4
May 1 - 7	Foremen	no data	0	0	1	0	3	0	0	4
	Men	no data	0	0	26	0	23	0	0	49
	Horses	no data	0	0	4	0	4	0	0	8
	Cars	no data	0	0	0	0	4	0	0	4
May 8 - 14	Foremen	no data	0	0	2	1	3	1	0	7
	Men	no data	0	0	33	13	23	7	0	76
	Horses	no data	0	0	4	0	4	0	0	8
	Cars	no data	0	0	0	2	2	0	0	4
May 15 - 21	Foremen	no data	0	0	2	1	3	0	1	7
	Men	no data	0	0	32	12	16	0	8	68
	Horses	no data	0	0	4	0	4	0	0	8
	Cars	no data	0	0	0	2	3	0	0	5

Date	Mile	7 - 8	8 - 9	9 - 10	10 - 11	11 - 12	12 - 13	13 - 14	14 - 15	TOTAL
May 22 - 31	Foremen	no data	0	0	0	3	2	0	0	5
	Men	no data	0	0	0	43	15	0	0	58
	Horses	no data	0	0	0	5	2	0	0	7
	Cars	no data	0	0	0	2	2	0	0	4
June 1 - 7	Foremen	no data	0	0	0	2	3	1	0	6
	Men	no data	0	0	0	35	27	6	0	68
	Horses	no data	0	0	0	4	3	2	0	9
	Cars	no data	0	0	0	0	0	0	0	0
June 8 - 14	Foremen	no data	0	0	0	2	3	no data	no data	5
	Men	no data	0	0	0	45	38	no data	no data	83
	Horses	no data	0	0	0	5	4	no data	no data	9
	Cars	no data	0	0	0	0	2	no data	no data	2
June 15 - 21	Foremen	no data	0	0	0	0	5	no data	no data	5
	Men	no data	0	0	0	0	68	no data	no data	68
	Horses	no data	0	0	0	0	3	no data	no data	3
	Cars	no data	0	0	0	0	0	no data	no data	0
June 22 - 30	Foremen	no data	0	0	0	0	5	no data	no data	5
	Men	no data	0	0	0	0	68	no data	no data	68
	Horses	no data	0	0	0	0	7	no data	no data	7
	Cars	no data	0	0	0	0	0	no data	no data	0

Compiled from Assistant Engineer's *Reports*, Penticton Museum & Archives

NUMBER OF MEN WORKING ON THE KVR
HYDRAULIC SUMMIT TO PENTICTON
JUNE 7, 1913 – JUNE 30, 1914
MILES 0 - 28 AND MILES 28 – 58

1913				1914		
	0-28	28-58			0-28	28-58
Jun 1–7:	865	149		Jan 1-7:	210	471
Jun 8–14:	888	1161		Jan 8-14:	232	448
Jun 15–21:	886	1148		Jan 15-21:	245	415
Jun 22–30:	916	1176		Jan 22-31:	232	380
Jul 1–7:	815	1186		Feb 1-7:	248	337
Jul 8–14:	786	1215		Feb 8-14:	234	324
Jul 15–21:	751	1201		Feb 15-21:	232	286
Jul 22–31:	748	1212		Feb 22-28:	202	271
Aug 1–7:	722	1211		Mar 1-7:	198	251
Aug 8–14:	697	1160		Mar 8-14:	192	231
Aug 15–21:	665	1146		Mar 15-21:	142	183
Aug 22–31:	656	1099		Mar 22-31:	133	154
Sept 1–7:	648	1041		Apr 1-7:	101	136
Sept 8–14:	682	1030		Apr 8-14:	54	134
Sept 15–21:	670	997		Apr 15-21:	54	128
Sept 22-30:	647	1046		Apr 22-30:	67	106
Oct 1-7:	616	1018		May 1-7:	60	41
Oct 8-14:	659	1034		May 8-14:	89	63
Oct 15-21:	646	1050		May 15-21:	75	0
Oct 22-31:	634	1032		May 22-31:	97	13
Nov 1-7:	605	1005		Jun 1-7:	106	0
Nov 8-14:	593	1030		Jun 8-14:	138	0
Nov 15-21:	557	981		Jun 15-21:	125	0
Nov 22-30:	490	883		Jun 22-30:	131	0
Dec 1-7:	383	821				
Dec 8-14:	306	731				
Dec 15-21:	285	605				
Dec 22-31:	238	515				

Compiled from Assistant Engineer's *Reports*, Penticton Museum & Archives

DEATHS DURING
THE CONSTRUCTION ERA
(HYDRAULIC SUMMIT TO PENTICTON)

CONSTRUCTION DEATHS

1. November 29, 1912
Louis Ericson, age 38
Location of death: Naramata
Cause: run over by teamster wagon

2. December 18 or 19, 1912
Louis Johnson
Location of death: Naramata (?)
Cause: premature explosion (thawing black powder)

3. March 15, 1913
E. Lundberg, age 40
Location of death: Four Mile Creek near Penticton
Cause: delayed explosion

4. Week of April 10, 1913
Walter Tauric (Greek)
Location of death: near Kelowna
Cause: unknown but while working

5. June 11, 1913
Camillo Allursio (Italian), age 32
Location of death: near Naramata
Cause: premature explosion

6. June 11, 1913
Dominic Allursio (Italian), age 22
Location of death: Naramata
Cause: premature explosion

7. June 11, 1913
J. P. (Pietre) Guiseppe (Italian)
Location of death: Naramata
Cause: premature explosion

8. July 24, 1913
Pete A.G. Anderson, age 35.
Location of death: Kimble's camp, Naramata
Cause: premature explosion (thawing dynamite)

9. August 8, 1913
Unknown (John Doe)
Location of death: Hildebrandt camp, Naramata
Cause: tunnel cave-in

10. August 8, 1913
Joe Cohn, age 35
Location of death: Hildebrandt camp, Naramata
Cause: tunnel cave-in

11. September 20, 1913
Carl Johnson, age 24
Location of death: Summit camp
Cause: pile driver accident

12. May 14, 1914
Henry Edward Kingzett, age 24
Location of death: Dibble's camp, Canyon Creek
Cause: fell off rock cut

13. April 21, 1914   Michal Borosliski, age 25
Location of death: Mile 29
Cause: pit cave in

14. May 20, 1914   Thomas Scott Barker, age 48
Location of death: near Penticton
Cause: trench cave-in

15. July 5, 1914   Henry Mathison, age 54
Location of death: Canyon Creek
Cause: knocked from trestle

16. July 18, 1914   Reginald McGee (McKee?), age 16
Location of death: Penticton
Cause: run over by train

17. August 14 or 15, 1914   Tom Buchanan
Location of death: Penticton
Cause: run over by train

OTHER DEATHS (natural, unrelated construction accidents or unknown)

18. August 19, 1912   John Johnson, age 38
Location of death: Penticton
Cause: fell from hotel fire escape

19. March 18 or 25, 1913   Leonardo Capusciuto
Location of death: near Morrissey's camp, Canyon Creek
Cause: froze (alcohol)

20. June 3, 1913   Ira Byrl Benedict, age 19
Location of death: Kelowna

21. July 22, 1913   Guiseppe Demarchi
Location of death: Kelowna

22. August 3, 1913   A. Boboff, age 24
Location of death: Okanagan Mission

23. prior to August 7, 1913   Unknown (John Doe) (young Russian)
Location of death: Okanagan Mission
Cause: typhoid fever (infected prior to work on KVR)

24. August 10, 1913   John Babitch, age 30
Location of death: Naramata

25. August 24, 1913   Peter Swanson, age 56
Location of death: Kelowna?

26. January 24, 1914   John Smith (Finn), age 46
Location of death: Naramata
Cause: acute peritonitis & heart condition

INDEX

IMPERIAL/METRIC CONVERSION CHART

1 foot = 0.3048 metres
1 metre = 3.28 feet or 39.37 inches
1 mile = 1.61 kilometre
1 kilometre = 0.62 miles